FERRY *POWERFUL*

A history of the modern British diesel ferry

by

Nick Robins

PREFACE

The world's first large diesel ferry was the **Ulster Monarch**. Although she was preceded by a number of relatively small petrol, paraffin and diesel units, the **Ulster Monarch** and her numerous sisters and cousins heralded the arrival of the now universally accepted marine diesel engine. The diesel has developed from the original slow speed direct reversing engines to the contemporary medium and high speed engines with reduction gears or controllable pitch propellers. The **Princess Victoria** was the first diesel driven car and passenger ferry, and this ship, and her post-war built namesake, were both sadly lost in tragic circumstances with heavy loss of life. Subsequently ships have grown in size and the massive vehicle and passenger ferries of today, the so-called cruise ferries, such as the **Ulysses** and **Pride of Hull**, now represent the current state of the art.

This book charts the expansion of the marine diesel on the British and Irish short sea routes. All the major motor driven units built before 1970 are described in detail, and the more important units built after that are also described. The story includes the trials and tribulations of these vessels, their crews and passengers. The war service of many of the diesel vessels is legion, and this account benefits greatly from the personal recollections of Ian Leafe, now aged 84, who was Junior Electrician aboard the **Ulster Monarch** during much of the Second World War.

As always with a book of this kind I am indebted to a number of friends who have helped gather information and helped to check the text. I am grateful to Alistair Deayton, Geoffrey Hamer, Willie Mackay, Justin Merrigan, Kevin Le Scelleur and John Stevenson, for a variety of information and data, but above all I am grateful to Ian Leafe. I am also indebted to both Ian Ramsay, Secretary of the Institution of Engineers and Shipbuilders in Scotland, and to Malcolm McRonald, himself an author of several shipping books, for checking and assisting in finalising the text. I must also record my debt of thanks to Gil Mayes for his thorough scrutiny of the text. All errors that remain are my own responsibility. Bernard McCall at *Coastal Shipping* and Sebright Printers have done a superb job in bringing the whole enterprise to conclusion - thanks to them.

Nick Robins
Crowmarsh, Oxfordshire

September 2003

Published by Bernard McCall, 400 Nore Road, Portishead, Bristol, BS20 8EZ, England.
Website : www.coastalshipping.co.uk
Telephone/fax : 01275 846178. E-mail : bernard@coastalshipping.co.uk
All distribution enquiries should be addressed to the publisher.

Printed by Sebright Printers, 12 - 18 Stokes Croft, Bristol, BS1 3PR
Telephone : 0117 942 5827; fax : 0117 942 0671
E-mail : info@sebright.co.uk
Website : www.sebright.co.uk

ISBN : 1-902953-10-X

The front cover illustrations depict the latest in diesel ferry design, along with what many now regard as a classic ferry of her generation.

Top left : P&O's **Pride of Hull** *as depicted on a company postcard which informs us that the ship covers the 197 nautical miles between Hull and Rotterdam with a maximum speed of 22 knots.* (P&O)

Top right : Irish Ferries' **Ulysses** *arriving at Dublin on 10 August 2003.* (John Southwood)

Bottom : One of the most popular locations for taking photographs used to be the pier at Folkestone. On a bright summer day, the **Vortigern** *makes a characteristically speedy approach to her berth.* (Bernard McCall)

CONTENTS

Chapter 1	SUCK-SQUEEZE-BANG-BLOW	4
Chapter 2	Petrol, paraffin and oil	10
Chapter 3	**Ulster Monarch** 3; **Innisfallen** 1	14
Chapter 4	The MacBrayne Lochs	21
Chapter 5	Irish Sea ferries and the international context	29
Chapter 6	Excursion ships and small ferries	36
Chapter 7	Paddle 'steamers'	42
Chapter 8	Post-war rebuilding	46
Chapter 9	Cargo with a few passengers	54
Chapter 10	Some little ships	68
Chapter 11	Single and twin screw classic ferries	76
Chapter 12	Twin and triple screw vehicle ferries	84
Chapter 13	Economies of scale	95
Chapter 14	Tales of old	101
Appendix 1	British and Irish new builds – small diesels, large diesels and turbine steamers	104
Appendix 2	Early development of two stroke and four stroke engines by Sulzer	105
Appendix 3	British and Irish motor ferries over 130 tons gross commissioned up to 1970	106
Ship Name Index		117

The **Mersey Coast** *of 1938 was built for the Coast Lines cargo service between Liverpool and Glasgow. She also served on the routes of the British Channel Islands Shipping Company.*

Except where credit is given otherwise, all photographs were taken by the author.

CHAPTER 1

SUCK-SQUEEZE-BANG-BLOW

It is hard to believe that there was ever anything other than the diesel engine. Watching the ebb and flow of ferry traffic off Southsea Castle on a summer evening evokes a wonderful illustration of the power of these engines, with the **Pride of Bilbao** arriving from the Continent, and the **Pride of Portsmouth** disappearing behind the Isle of Wight. At the same time, the small grey-hulled steamer **Shieldhall** comes into view from the opposite direction. The contrast is extreme. The diminutive, now preserved, former sludge carrier from the Clyde gently glides forward on an evening excursion out of Southampton, with steam hissing from beneath the auxiliary machinery on the forecastle. The mighty cross-channel ferry, her diesel engines audible as she passes the castle, looking businesslike, but majestic, in her P&O blue livery, pushes into the harbour against the tide. Her Promenade Deck is alive with holiday-makers returning from France, below are cars, coaches and lorries, the latter laden with goods to sustain the nation.

The history of the motor ferry and the associated inshore and coastal passenger ships is an interesting and exciting story. Nowadays, the diesel engine or oil engine is the ubiquitous norm for shipping of all shapes and sizes, but this has only been the case for the last few decades (Appendix 1). The diesel engine struggled hard to gain acceptance in short sea trades throughout the first half of the twentieth century. At first the engines were not powerful enough and were too slow for ferry traffic, but more recently they have acquired reduction gearing for the more modern high speed engines. Slow in arriving, the internal combustion engine has taken over completely and all our ferries are now diesel driven.

At the beginning of the twentieth century the steam reciprocating engine, in all its different forms, powered all the short sea ferries around our coasts. Steel-hulled ships driven by propellers, or the less efficient side wheel or paddle wheel, had replaced iron and wooden hulled vessels. The water tube boiler was becoming available to provide higher operating pressures, and Mr Charles Parsons was about to release his newly invented steam turbine engine into the short sea world with his prototype, the Clyde excursion steamer **King Edward**. In a country where coal and labour were cheap, and where ferry operators were satisfied with steam power, the time was wholly inappropriate for the new, and essentially foreign-developed, technology of the internal combustion engine and its liquid fuel.

Nicolas August Otto and his colleague Gottlieb Daimler had developed the four-stroke cycle spark ignition engine in the 1870s. Better known as the petrol engine, its development was carried out at the Gasmotoreufabrik Deutz factory in Cologne which soon came to be the largest manufacturer of internal combustion engines in the world. School-boy mechanics will recall the principle of this engine from the words SUCK-SQUEEZE-BANG-BLOW, or more conventionally, an air and fuel INDUCTION stroke moving outwards from the cylinder head, COMPRESSION of the charge with an inward stroke, the outward POWER stroke, and finally the inward EXHAUST stroke. This engine normally has four cylinders so that a single power stroke is driving the crankshaft every half rotation.

Eagle Steamers **Golden Eagle** *(1909) was a large excursion paddle steamer of the early 20th century. After a career of 40 years, she was replaced by the motor ship* **Queen of the Channel** *(1949).*

(Author's collection)

During the 1880s and 1890s a number of workers, including Rudolf Diesel and Herbert Akroyd-Stuart, were working on another engine known as the four-stroke cycle compression ignition engine, nowadays referred to as the diesel engine. Heavy oils need to be vaporized, whereas petrol, with a lower flash point, vaporizes readily on contact with warm air in the engine's carburettor. The main difference with the diesel engine is that it does not use an ignition spark to burn the fuel but rather the heat generated from compressing the gas and vaporised fuel during the compression stroke. The vaporization process combines heat and turbulence, which may include a fine spray of fuel across a hot bulb, and the injection of compressed air. Early oil engines had a single cylinder only.

The first reliable oil engine was built in the workshops of Mashinenfabrik Augsburg Nürnburg (better known by the abbreviation MAN) in 1897. Compressed air was supplied by a compressor driven by the shaft. To start the engine an auxiliary compressor was required and the air flow was controlled by a cam and rocking levers. Early engines of this type were fuelled by naphtha, shale oil and even household lamp oil.

The high-speed petrol engine-driven motor boat was first demonstrated at the 1889 Paris Exhibition. It was not long before the motor boat acquired a military role. However, paraffin was substituted for petroleum in slower speed engines, as this fuel had a slightly lower flash point and was considered to be safer at sea. Indeed it was paraffin which fuelled the first commercial internal combustion engined ferries with the three Edwardian 'steamers' **Comet**, **Scout** and **Lochinvar** operated in western Scotland by David MacBrayne Limited (Chapter 2).

Early marine oil engines comprised one or more cylinders coupled to a reversible pitch propeller. The first was a 15 kW 2-cylinder unit on a canal barge. These applications were all pioneered by the Russians and were mainly used on fishing boats. The 4-cylinder marine oil engine was used in increasingly larger vessels throughout the Edwardian period and was successively utilised on ships up to 500 tons displacement. Uses included barges, tugs and some small harbour ferries and workboats. The critical advantage of the diesel engine was that it could be operated efficiently at a variety of different loads. It was quickly realised that the oil engine suited marine use better than the spark-ignition engine as the longer connecting rod, or piston, provided greater torque against less power.

The breakthrough for the marine diesel came in 1910 when the **Selandia** was completed for Det Østasiatiske Kompagni. She had two diesel engines, each providing a power output of 1100 kW, but these were the first marine diesels to be designed to the basic principles we know today, and not based merely on conventional steam reciprocating engine technology as was the case with early marine diesels. These were the very first long-stroke, cross-head type enclosed direct-reversible engines. By way of an advertisement for the motor engine, the **Selandia** carried no funnel. The **Selandia** was 113 m long by 16 m broad, and with her twin engines provided a combined power of 1870 kW at 140 revolutions per minute; she could maintain a speed of 11 knots (a modern marine diesel can typically provide at least twice this power). The engines were four stroke, 8-cylinder engines, each with a bore of 520 mm and a stroke of 720 mm. The air blast pressure was 450 kg. The design was a great success and two sister ships quickly followed, one of which, the **Jutlandia**, was built and engined by Barclay, Curle Ltd, on the Clyde, in 1911.

There were other ships. The **Suecia**, for example, was the first Swedish ocean-going diesel ship and she had twin 8-cylinder four stroke single action Burmeister & Wain (B&W) type engines. However, in those early days, the motor ship was slightly more expensive to run than the conventional steamer, and successful operation depended on fuel oil being available at regular ports of call. Though more expensive, and also requiring a higher degree of training for the engine room staff, the motor ships proved their worth, as the engines and the bunker spaces were smaller and lighter, and more payload could be carried. A series of motor coasters built just prior to 1914 for Paton & Hendry, and given Innis- names, was doomed by the shortage of trained engineering staff. However, by 1930 the average motor ship was using only one third of the fuel for the equivalent output of an oil engined turbine steamer and its prospects for the coasting industry were greatly improved.

The efficiency of the marine internal combustion engine benefited greatly from research into its use for submarines. Development went through a series of hybrids, of which the oddest was perhaps the so called fast attack K-Class submarines developed in the Great War. These boats had twin steam turbines, which could drive them on the surface at 24 knots, auxiliary diesel engines for use before and after diving, and electric motors for limited use when submerged.

Then there was the world's first ocean going motor passenger liner, Elder Dempster Line's **Aba**. She was originally ordered from Barclay, Curle and Company by the Russian Tsarist Government, but during the Russian Revolution in 1917, construction was stopped and she was completed the following year for the Glen Line as the **Glenapp**. The Glen Line had already switched completely to the B &W type engine after receiving the **Glenartney** and **Glenamoy** from Harland and Wolff in Belfast in 1915 and 1916, never thereafter to build another steamship. In 1921, the **Glenapp** was acquired by Elder Dempster and rebuilt as a passenger liner for their West African service. Her engines comprised two 8-cylinder four stroke single action B&W type diesels built by Harland & Wolff. The cylinders had a bore of 780 mm and a stroke of 1100 mm and they drove twin screws with an output of 3580 kW at 120 revolutions per minute – the **Aba** was the most powerful motorship of her day. A highly successful ship, she was joined by a new build, the **Adda**, in 1922 - see page 9.

By the 1920s, the marine diesel was considered as a viable alternative to the steam turbine engine and the steam reciprocating engine. The following description by A C Hardy first appeared as part of an article entitled "The Ship's Engines" in the *The Wonder Book of Ships* published in that period:

"The majority of marine internal combustion engines, or diesel engines, as they are generally called, are single acting, but recently many vessels have been fitted with double-acting internal combustion engines. The advantages of this type over the single-acting engine are many, because it means that one cylinder can do what two cylinders did formerly, and hence roughly the number of cylinders for the same power can be halved.

Diesel engines are built either on the 'four stroke cycle' or upon the 'two stroke cycle' (see Appendix 2). In the former there is a power impulse on one side of the piston once every two revolutions of the crank, and in the latter, by a different arrangement of valves, a power impulse is made once every revolution.

There are two distinct services of compressed air in diesel-engined ships. One of which, supplied usually by a compressor driven off a forward extension of the crank shaft, is used in most engines for injecting fuel into the cylinders at high pressure and the other, supplied by steam or electric-driven compressors on the engine room floor, for starting up the engine and for manoeuvring it.

There are many specialised makes of diesel engines, all of which do the same thing in a slightly different manner. Diesel engines are now largely used for all classes of ship except certain naval vessels and very high-speed mercantile vessels, for which purposes the geared turbine still holds the field."

The old air blast engines have long been superseded, but the basic principle of the diesel remains unchanged. The marine steam engines have now almost entirely been replaced by diesel for most purposes, although diesel-electric propulsion is now seen as a useful drive couple for specialist uses such as cruise ships and other large vessels. Air blast fuel injection engines were still built as late as the 1930s, but are now long overtaken by airless engines, with solid fuel injection into the cylinders at very high pressures. The early airless engines were medium speed engines, running at between 400 and 700 revolutions per minute and coupled to fluid couplings and reverse/reduction gearboxes. Nowadays, higher speed engines are in use. However, the starter compresser and pressure vessel are still essential components of the engine room.

Direct reversible engines needed to be shut down and restarted with compressed air once the reversing cam was moved into position. This was no mean feat in a tideway and a strong wind (e.g. the **Winchester**, see Chapter 9). These engines were introduced because gear cutting technology was still in its infancy and clutches had not been developed to take the high torques. Whenever the propeller was required to reverse direction, the engine was stopped, like a steam one, and restarted in the opposite rotation. The camshaft had two sets of cams on it, one set for the ahead events and the other for astern. To change direction the camshaft was slid from the ahead to the reverse position (or vice versa), the engine was then turned over with compressed air whilst at the same time fuel was injected until the engine fired. When this happened the air was shut off and the fuel supply increased to attain the required revolutions. Nowadays, reduction gears (for the higher speed engines) and controllable pitch propellers control direction and speed of the ship.

In the original four stroke engine, the first stroke draws in the air, the second stroke (up) compresses it, during the third stroke fuel oil is injected, and the fourth stroke (again up) is the exhaust stroke. The more sophisticated two stroke engine has a first stroke (the power stroke) but in this engine there are two ports at the bottom of the cylinder. These are opened by the piston to allow the exhaust to escape, while on the other side of the cylinder, air from an auxiliary compressor is admitted to sweep the exhaust gases out. The following up stroke compresses the air again (as in the second up stroke of the four stroke engine). The cycle is then repeated with fuel oil injected into the cylinder on the next down stroke. Both engine systems require compressed air to be injected into at least one cylinder to get the engine turning and to start the combustion process.

Early experiments with diesel-electric propulsion for short sea vessels, such as the David MacBrayne vessel **Lochfyne** (Chapter 4), were a logical development in parallel with the turbo-electric systems aboard the

P&O liner *Viceroy of India*. But what made the London & North Eastern Railway order a diesel-electric paddle ship, the *Talisman*, in 1935 (Chapter 7)? More innovative, but this time highly successful, was the Voith Schneider propelling machinery installed on the pre-war diesel powered Isle of Wight ferry *Vecta* (Chapter 6).

The mother of the diesel driven cross channel ferry was the *Ulster Monarch* completed by Harland & Wolff in 1929 (Chapter 3, see also Appendix 3). She was the world's very first large motor ferry. The *Ulster Monarch* and her two immediate sisters were so successful on the overnight Belfast to Liverpool run that they became the standard basic design for Coast Lines Seaway group of companies for the next quarter century (Table 1). The group also adopted diesel propulsion in all its new passenger units for the David MacBrayne fleet from 1930 onwards (Chapter 4). It was then customary to fit diesel engines only to the smaller coastal units and two stroke direct reversing engines such as Sulzer, British Polar, Atlas and Widdop were commonplace. These engines were heavy and low powered and ran at slow speeds. However, the greatest exponent of the fast cross channel ferry in the 1930s was the Belgian State Marine service.

With the exception of the London, Midland & Scottish Railway's two ferries named *Princess Victoria*, such innovation was not part of the Railway shipping fleet philosophy, nor that of the Isle of Man Steam Packet Company. Those ferry operators stuck doggedly to steam turbine machinery whilst others were ahead in both machinery and overall ship design, not least with regard to roll-on roll-off capability. This remained the case into the 1980s, when competition on the Heysham to Douglas route, and independent operators such as Townsend Brothers at Dover, finally forced this traditionalism off the agenda.

Before the Second World War the most powerful oil engines used the double acting principle. These had very vulnerable lower con rods and glands, which could only be serviced by stripping down the whole of the engine. During the war years, most manufacturers switched to single acting two stoke cross-head type engines, providing simpler construction, easier maintenance and economy of fuel. The two most popular British designs in post-war years were the Doxford opposed piston, uniflow-scavenging two stroke engine and the Harland & Wolff opposed piston engine. Subsequent increases in power by up to 40% have been achieved by turbo-charging, the first marine turbo-charged diesel going to sea aboard a Danish tanker in 1952.

The first diesel vehicle ferry, the **Bardic Ferry** *(1957) is seen approaching the lock at Preston in September 1968.*

The **Free Enterprise III** *(1966), seen off Dover in July 1968, was one of the new generation of diesel car ferries deployed at Dover by Townsend Brothers Ferries.*

*The brand new **Innisfallen** arrives at the Swansea terminal from Cork in June 1969. She represented the state of the art at the end of the 1960s.*

From the 1950s onwards, the medium speed four stroke diesel engine began to be developed to give higher power outputs suitable for the larger ferries of the day. The engines were either direct reversing, coupled through a reversing gearbox, or non-reversing with controllable pitch propellers which could reverse the thrust. The early diesel engines were naturally aspirated, but this was followed by mechanical scavenging of the cylinders and subsequently by turbo blowers and intercoolers. Careful design and use of specially developed alloys has allowed the power to weight ratio to increase dramatically in recent years, there now being in-line and vee engines, with some driving direct to the propellers and others via gearboxes. There has also been a move towards burning boiler grade fuel rather than distillates, but careful pre-treatment of the fuel is needed before it is burnt.

Thus, where the old diesel ferries, especially the smaller ones, were once fitted with direct-reversing, slow speed engines, they now have either a medium speed or high speed engine driving through a reduction gearbox. Reverse thrust is now achieved either via a reverse reduction gear or by a controllable pitch propeller in conjunction with reduction gears. The engines to this day, with very few exceptions, still require compressed air to start.

The steam turbine engine is still preferred for use in some very large liquid-gas carriers in which the gas discharge, or boil-off, from the cargo can be economically used to fuel the boilers. For all other purposes, the economy of the modern marine diesel or oil engine makes it supreme for both deep sea and coastal services. The last of the steam turbine ferries in service in UK waters was the ***Ben-my-Chree***, which served on the Isle of Man routes until 1985, finally driven out of service by spiralling fuel costs. This then is the story of the slow encroachment of the diesel engine on our ferry, coastal and excursion shipping during the twentieth century, and of the inevitable demise of the steam engine.

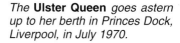

*The **Ulster Queen** goes astern up to her berth in Princes Dock, Liverpool, in July 1970.*

BEFORE THE *SELANDIA*

Before the **Selandia**, the engines were designed around steam reciprocating technology and the engine rooms looked little different from the conventional power units of the day. The first commercial motor vessel was the triple screw tanker **Vandal**, built and engined by Nobel Brothers of Petersburg in 1904 for use on the Caspian Sea. Her engines were non-reversible and were coupled to electric drive giving 300 kW, a coupling again used, but on bigger vessels, from the 1930s onwards. The availability of appropriate oil distillates in the Caspian and Volga region was an essential driver to Russian innovation at this time.

In 1910 the Dutch built the tanker **Vulcanus**, the very first deep sea motor ship. She had 6-cylinder four stroke Werkspoor engines which could develop 375 kW. The cylinders had a bore of 400 mm and a stroke of 600 mm and, running at 180 revolutions per minute, they could drive the 1910 tons displacement of the vessel at 8.4 knots. The engines were based on steam reciprocating technology, and included all steam driven auxiliaries, pumps and scavengers. The crank pit was open in these early engines, so that the engineers (who mistrusted the new technology) could still see the bearings. There were two separate cam shafts that could be brought into play so that these direct-drive engines were fully reversible. Similar ships were the Newcastle built **Toiler** of 1911 and the **Juno** of 1912.

By 1911 it is estimated (see Guthrie, 1971) that there were:

Tankers :
12 Russian on the Volga and Caspian; maximum power of any of these vessels was 900 kW.
4 German, the most powerful of 3100 kW.
1 British – 600 kW. 1 American on the Great Lakes.

Tugs :
22 Russian, 13 others.

Cargo ships :
9 Russian, 7 German, 7 Scandinavian, 4 Dutch, 3 British, 2 Swiss, 2 Congolese.

There were also about 30 warships, 115 submarines, plus about 30 fishing vessels and others. All were dependent on the availability of adequate fuel supplies on the normal routes and service areas. There were no oil-engined ferries. All were subject to frequent break down and regular repair.

Elder Dempster Line's **Adda** (1922), one of the very first diesel passenger liners.

(National Maritime Museum)

CHAPTER 2

PETROL, PARAFFIN AND OIL

Pioneer of the internal combustion engine on UK inshore and coastal passenger services was David MacBrayne Limited. Conscious of the time needed to prepare a steam engine for service, and of the cost of banking down fires in the evening ready for early morning starts and full steam, this Scottish operator bought its first motor driven ship as early as 1907. She was a small vessel of some 43 tons gross which revived the name of Henry Bell's very first steamship on the Clyde, that of **Comet**. The motorship **Comet** was built by Robertson of Canning Town as the **Win**, and she came into the MacBrayne fleet when two years old. Her twin 4-cylinder paraffin-fuelled motors produced 90 kW. They were made at Manchester by L Gardner & Sons.

The **Comet** had a straight stem and a counter stern. There were two separate deck houses with an open bridge on top of the after deckhouse. A single lifeboat was slung over the stern. There was ample covered accommodation below decks. Duckworth and Langmuir (see references) write:

"Travelling on board was a very different experience from that on a steamer, as the engine noises were apt to be rather tiresome. Early in her service the popping of the exhaust was dreadful, but this was afterwards largely rectified by improving silencing".

Nevertheless the little ship proved highly successful. Her paraffin engines served her until 1928 when they were replaced during a major refurbishment which followed a serious grounding near Fort Matilda. Her new engines were also built by Gardner, and were 8-cylinder diesels, which provided an increased output of 107 kW. The little ship continued to serve her owners until 1947, when she was sold; her hull is still in use today as the houseboat **Gradely** at Shoreham. She had seen service on a variety of inshore routes, including the Crinan Canal, but her main employment had been on the Clyde as the Lochgoil mail ship. Ironically she was replaced by a steamer when she finally left the Clyde.

Given experience with the **Comet**, MacBraynes also commissioned a full size 'steamer', the **Scout**, in 1907, and she too was equipped with paraffin engines. These were built at Bristol by the Griffin Engineering Company, of Bath, and were installed in the ship by her builders, the Ailsa Shipbuilding Company of Troon. Her twin engines were of the four stroke cycle single acting type and produced 195 kW. Each engine had four cylinders with a bore of 280 mm and a stroke of 330 mm. The **Scout** was altogether a much larger ship than the **Comet** and had a gross tonnage of 82 and a length of 30 metres.

The **Scout** worked the Ballachulish to Kinlochleven service. Outwardly she looked like the typical inshore steamer of the day, but only after a small funnel was added shortly after she entered service. She was particularly well endowed with promenade space given her small tonnage. Unhappily, after a career of only six years, the **Scout** was destroyed by fire. This was the result of a serious blow-back from her engines which occurred in August 1913, one of the first recorded marine accidents to have resulted from the malfunction of an internal combustion engine. The ship's two lifeboats were salved and fitted on the paddle steamer **Columba** until she was scrapped, when they were transferred to the turbine steamer **King George V**.

The third motorship to join the MacBrayne fleet was something of an unsung hero, alas, with a very sad end. This was the **Lochinvar**, which was built in 1908 by Scott & Sons, of Bowling, and engined by L Gardner & Sons. This time, three 6-cylinder single acting paraffin engines were used to produce 215 kW to drive the ship via three independent shafts. The three engine system was not used again until the **Free Enterprise IV** was commissioned for Townsend Brothers in 1969. The **Lochinvar** was initially measured at 188 gross tons, and her required service speed was 8 knots. The new motor ship was placed on the Oban to Tobermory mail service as a direct replacement for the elderly iron-hulled paddle steamer **Carabinier**. The dining saloon sported a series of eight panels depicting the exciting life of young Lochinvar.

Originally the **Lochinvar** had one tall and very thin funnel near the stern, but this was soon replaced by three separate stove-pipes, one for each engine. These pipes were later diverted to a short funnel just before the cargo hold, where there was an electrically driven crane, the funnel being particularly short to allow the crane to operate over the top of it. Not a very attractive looking ship, she was nevertheless highly successful on her daily year-round run up the Sound of Mull. Only very rarely was she called upon to relieve elsewhere.

Her prototype marine paraffin engines were replaced in 1926 when she received three new 6-cylinder Gardner 'heavy oil' diesel engines coupled independently, as before, to her triple screws. Her new engines were similar to those fitted in **Lochearn** and **Lochmor** (Chapter 4), and this uniformity assisted with the availability of spares, which lavishly included a spare engine for each of the three ships. The engines were direct reversing two stroke, each with a cylinder bore of 242 mm and a stroke of 272 mm. Following the Second World War, the **Lochinvar** received a major refurbishment and a third set of engines made by Davey-Paxman of Colchester. At this stage she was reduced from triple screw to twin screw, requiring only two engines. These were 6-cylinder, in-line, four stroke engines, which were connected to the shafts via Modern Wheel Drive reverse/reduction gearboxes. The engines were placed under an acoustic hood, somewhat akin to a large dog kennel, and only when this was in place was it possible to travel on the ship without being overwhelmed by the dreadful noise of the engines. A third engine was maintained ashore, as replacement.

The **Lochinvar** completed her last run up and down the Sound of Mull in May 1960 and was laid up at Shandon by Timbacraft Ltd, who were then temporarily registered as her owners. She was quickly resold to the Thames & Medway Navigation Company and renamed **Anzio I**. For the next three summers, she plied

successfully between Sheerness and Southend, on the Thames, with capacity for 351 excursion passengers. She always looked very small when viewed from the Promenade Deck of the Pier at Southend and even seemed small alongside the paddler **Medway Queen**, which was herself not a large vessel. To the end, she portrayed a workmanlike image, never attracting the acclaim deserved of such an innovative vessel. Indeed, few at the end of the pier would even give her a second glance in the presence of the **Medway Queen**.

The veteran **Lochinvar** *(1908) seen in Scotland at Mallaig in 1959 towards the end of her career.* *(National Maritime Museum)*

The career of the **Anzio I** came to an abrupt end when Sheerness Harbour withdrew access to the ship. She was then laid up, and in 1966 was sold to Cromarty Cruises for a new service between Inverness and Invergordon. Sadly, the elderly ship was driven ashore two days out of the Thames on the passage north. She foundered at Donna Nook, near the Humber mouth, with the loss of her entire crew of thirteen. Media coverage of the loss failed to identify the ship as a significant part of our maritime heritage. Nonetheless, David Hope MacBrayne and Laurence MacBrayne must be commended on their wisdom and foresight when they originally sanctioned the building of the ship.

The **Lochinvar** and the **Scout** must be remembered as Britain's pioneer motor-driven sea-going passenger units. They were both immensely successful on the routes for which they had been designed, but both suffered throughout much of their career from excessive engine noise in the passenger spaces and on deck. The long service life of both the **Lochinvar** (58 years) and the earlier **Comet** (40 years) is testimony to sound design and construction, although not to their original engines. The inadequacies of the paraffin engine, of course, had been highlighted by the premature loss of the **Scout** at the tender age of only six years.

As so often was the case in the twentieth century, war provided opportunity for engineering innovation and development. The needs of the submariner were the catalyst for developing the marine diesel engine, so that by the end of the Great War the efficiency and reliability of heavy oil marine engines (the paraffin engine was now no longer considered viable) were attractive to an increasing number of deep-sea operators. The appeal was less in the short-sea area, where services required fast speeds which were then best served by the turbine or even conventional reciprocating machinery.

Resistance to the new internal combustion engine was compounded by the major operators of cross-channel services, then, and for many years yet to come, dominated by the many regional railways. Preference for steam traction was, of course, only natural on a steam driven railway. Concession to the oil engine was at first only for very small units. For example, the Great Eastern Railway commissioned three small motor boats between 1910 and 1914 to operate the Shotley, Harwich Pier and Felixstowe Dock ferry service. The first was the **Pin Mill**, which was built at Ipswich, followed by the **Epping** and **Hainault**, which were built by Vosper at Portsmouth. Although they were all of different hull sizes, each had a small oil engine capable of providing 15 kW. The original trio was followed in 1925 by the **Brightlingsea**, which retained her original 60 kW engines until 1983, before retiring to seasonal excursion use two years later.

Other small diesel ferries were built for a variety of services throughout the 1920s. Typical, was the pair of wooden hulled diesel powered boats built at Dartmouth, the **Berry Castle** and **Dittisham Castle**, for the River Dart Steamboat Company in 1922. These little ships were of only 13 tons gross.

The first Kyle to Kyleakin turntable ferry was built in 1930. The turntable ferry had already been proven at Ballachulish before the wooden-hulled petrol-engined **Kyleakin** was delivered from her builders, Webster & Bickerton of Goole. The engine had four cylinders, and was built by Kelvin-Ricardo. Subsequent ships of this type built between 1936 and 1951 had 3-cylinder Gleniffer diesels, and all but one had steel hulls. Each could accommodate one or two cars plus up to 100 passengers.

The first diesel ferries of any significant proportions were built for the Southern Railway for their new Portsmouth to Fishbourne, Isle of Wight, vehicular service. The first pair of new ferries was the **Fishbourne**, completed in 1927 at a cost of £13,350, and the **Wootton**, which followed a year later to a slightly enlarged design and cost £17,300. A third vessel, the **Hilsea**, was completed in 1930.

Dendy Marshall records the new service in *A History of the Southern Railway* (see reference section):

"In July 1927 a new departure was set up by the inauguration, between Portsmouth Harbour and Fishbourne in Wootton Creek in the Isle of Wight, of a ferry boat service for the conveyance, in particular, of motor cars. The new service – which replaced transit by tow boats – necessitated the construction of a slipway at Fishbourne, with a reinforced concrete road, 300 yards long. The **Fishbourne**, built by Denny Brothers, is 125 feet (38 m) long overall, has a beam of 25 feet (8 m), and is of the double-ended type. Accommodation is provided for sixteen to twenty cars, in two rows, and there is a ladies' and a gentlemen's saloon. A hinged platform at each end allows for variation in tide-level; and cars pass off the boat at the opposite end to that by which they entered, and can at once proceed on their journey. The motive power is supplied by two sets of semi-diesel engines, made by Norris, Henty & Gardner, which drive independent propellers and furnish a speed of 8 knots."

The three ships were all built by William Denny of Dumbarton. They had twin propellers and twin rudders at each end. The twin 4-cylinder two-cycle single action Gardner diesel engines provided 180 kW to drive these somewhat dumpy vessels along. Comparable power available to the rather sleeker passenger paddle steamers of that era on the Solent was generally less than 150 kW. However, the new vehicular ferries were small by today's standards, the **Fishbourne** having a capacity of only 136 tons gross and her younger sisters of 149 tons gross. In their later years, the **Fishbourne** could carry up to 16 cars and the larger pair about 20. The three prototype ferries were, however, hugely successful and were only displaced from the Portsmouth fleet in 1961.

*The **Fishbourne** (1927) on the stocks prior to launch at William Denny's yard in Dumbarton.*

(National Maritime Museum)

A small turntable vehicle ferry, with accommodation for just four cars, was completed for the London, Midland & Scottish Railway's Kyle to Kyleakin, Skye, ferry service in 1930. The first of many motor driven turntable ferries on this route (side loading to a slipway), the **Kyleakin** came from the yard of Webster & Bickerton of Goole, and interestingly reverted to the petrol engine to drive her single screw. It was a 4-cylinder engine which developed 27 kW. Existing motor launches on the route were then powered by paraffin engines. The **Kyleakin** was displaced from Kyle in 1951, but continued in service between Glenelg and Kylerhea until she was sunk off Broadford in a storm in 1959. The next vessel for the route, the **Moil**, which was built in 1936, had a 3-cylinder Gleniffer diesel unit.

As late as 1934 two paraffin-engined wooden launches, the **Lady Ailsa** and the **Carrick Lass**, were built for excursion services out of Girvan. Paraffin engines were then still widely used to power auxiliary equipment on larger ferries, but were now rarely used as the main engine.

Whilst the Southern Railway had commissioned three small oil-engined vehicle ferries, and the London, Midland & Scottish Railway had reverted to the petrol engine in the late 1920s, others were already stealing a march. Coast Lines were busy designing the large **Ulster Monarch**-class passenger and cargo ferries for their prestigious overnight Liverpool to Belfast service, and their associate company, David MacBrayne, was well advanced with the design of diesel-driven inter-island ferries. Indeed, the diesel engine was about to have a major impact on short sea services everywhere, although the Railways continued to pretend that steam was the only viable source of marine motive power for some time yet to come.

The influence of the diesel engine on deep sea services was already profound. Indeed, the first three major diesel driven liner casualties happened in quick succession in the early 1930s. The **Highland Hope**, a brand new unit in the Nelson Line was wrecked in dense fog in 1930, the six year old Burns Philip liner **Malabar** hit the rocks off Sydney soon after (giving her name to the suburb of Sydney now called Malabar), and the four year old Furness Withy cruise liner **Bermuda** burnt out at her berth in New York in June 1931. Not only had the motor ship arrived, it was in the news too.

*The **Lochalsh** (1957) waiting to load at the Kyle of Lochalsh slip in August 1964.*

CHAPTER 3

ULSTER MONARCH 3; INNISFALLEN 1

After the Great War, the Liverpool to Belfast night ferry service of the Belfast Steamship Company was operated by three steamers. These were the **Graphic** and **Heroic**, which dated from 1906, and the slightly larger **Patriotic** which had been completed in 1912. The three ship service was required for a nightly departure from both ports because, at that time, tidal conditions often required the steamer to handle passengers at the Princes Landing Stage at Liverpool, then to wait for access to their berth in the dock system. A fourth steamer, the **Classic**, which had been built in 1893, was available to cover refits until she was chartered to the City of Cork Steam Packet Company in the summer of 1921. These were very much traditional ships driven by conventional steam reciprocating machinery, although the **Graphic** and **Heroic** were unusual in having quadruple expansion machinery, rather than the more normal triple expansion scheme used in the **Patriotic**. They were, however, comfortable ships and were popular with the travelling public despite their increasing age in post-war years.

An order for three replacement ferries was placed with Harland & Wolff in the late 1920s. Although consideration had at one time been given to re-equipping the earlier **Graphic** and **Heroic** with the new turbine machinery then making inroads into cross-channel traffic, no such consideration was given to the design of their successors. The outcome was the first diesel-driven cross-channel passenger ferry in the world, the **Ulster Monarch**. She and her two sisters, the **Ulster Queen** and **Ulster Prince**, were each equipped with two 10-cylinder Burmeister & Wain type diesels with four stroke single acting trunk pistons of the airless injection type. The cylinders were 360 mm bore with 980 mm stroke and at 1600 revolutions per minute they developed 5600 kW giving the ship a service speed of 18 knots. Although the two stroke cycle engine had already been tried at sea, the proven four stroke principle was adopted. However, these were the first airless injection engines to be made at Belfast. The **Ulster Monarch** started her commercial life in 1929, whilst her sisters were delayed in the builder's yard until the following year by a joiners' strike.

*The railway companies stayed loyal to steam:the 25-knot steam turbine ferry **Brighton** (1931) was built for the Southern Railway's Newhaven - Dieppe route at the time when the **Ulster Monarch** and her sisters were commissioned.*

(Mike Walker collection)

There were a number of reasons why diesel power was almost an inevitability for the three new ships. The Belfast Steamship Company had been taken over by the Coast Lines Group in 1919. Although the company had then lost its financial independence, it had temporally gained an element of security in the immediate post-war years. However, as time progressed, that financial security became more tenuous as the mighty Royal Mail Group, parent of Coast Lines, became less and less financially viable.

The Royal Mail Group included three shipbuilders, one of which was the local Belfast company Harland & Wolff. At that time, Harland & Wolff was heavily committed to diesel machinery and was building a succession of large passenger liners, each equipped with Burmeister & Wain type engines constructed locally under licence. Many of these were internal orders within the Royal Mail Group and included ships for Royal Mail Line, Union-Castle Line and the Nelson Line. The **Britannic** and **Georgic** were also in the design offices at that time. Indeed, it was almost certainly the Nelson Line's **Highland Monarch**, launched at Belfast in May 1928, which sowed the seed of the new nomenclature for the three ferries.

The commercial need for Harland & Wolff to demonstrate the viability of diesel power for fast ferries, coupled with the need for the Royal Mail Group to retain the business of ship replacement in house, was compelling. Yard numbers 695, 696 and 697 were laid down respectively on 1 March, 3 March and 22 March 1928. Estimated building costs for the three ships was £261, 000 for the first, £259, 000 for the next and £255, 000 for the third vessel. In order to retain independence from the ailing Royal Mail Group, the necessary finance was raised as a mortgage from the Bank of Ireland. As it turned out, the mortgage was totally redeemed by 1936, reflecting the success of these ships in what were at best commercially difficult times.

The three Ulster sisters were nearly identical with classical three island type hulls and two squat funnels (the fore funnel was a dummy). Their hulls were 105 m long by 14 m broad and they measured 3735 tons gross, although the **Ulster Monarch**, sole survivor of the Second World War, was remeasured at 3799 tons gross in 1946. They were given attractive cruiser style sterns that provided a modern image when compared with the traditional counter sterns still in vogue at that time. They wore the classic red and black funnel colours which complemented their grey hulls to present an image not unlike the liners **Britannic** and **Georgic**, and similar also to the ships of the Union Castle Line. The mini-liner image was further enhanced by the row of four white lifeboats slung beneath gravity davits on either side of the midships superstructure.

The three ships had very high standard passenger accommodation for 419 saloon and 100 steerage class passengers, although many more passengers were carried unberthed. The saloon or first class accommodation comprised a vertical block in the central part of the superstructure and cabin accommodation was spread over the four decks A (Promenade Deck), B, C and D. Cabins were mainly single and two berth, and some internal cabins had the Bibby-type alleyway leading to a porthole. All had hot and cold running water and there were four state-rooms which also had showers and toilets. There was a smoke room and bar on the Promenade Deck. This was in the Tudor style with an arched roof, trusses and oak panelling with galleon type windows to give an impression of the country house. The lounge was furnished in grey wood panels on A Deck with an open deck space either side of it, and the restaurant was on B Deck, aft of the Purser's office. The restaurant was panelled in heavy mahogany with pink curtains and drapes in the style of Louis XVI. Individual tables set for twos and fours were each adorned with a pink shaded lamp. Interestingly the public rooms were normally only used for about three hours each night and the dining room for a further one hour in the morning for breakfasts.

Steerage class accommodation was situated aft on the poop on B and C Decks. There was a lounge, bar, a large cafeteria and a dining saloon and cabin accommodation was arranged in multiple berths. Each ship carried a policeman (an ex-Liverpool city police constable) whose job was to keep order.

The ships could each handle about 700 tons of cargo. Cargo was distributed between two holds, one forward and one aft of the superstructure. The forward hold and 'tween deck space was served by two hatches, the after hold by one, and the ship's own derricks and electric winches handled much of the cargo. A generator set of 110 kW provided the power for these. The daytime layover offered plenty of time for cargo handling, except when the tides at Liverpool prevented access to the dockside until late morning.

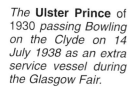

The **Ulster Prince** of 1930 *passing Bowling on the Clyde on 14 July 1938 as an extra service vessel during the Glasgow Fair.*

(Alistair Deayton collection)

The **Ulster Monarch** sailed on her maiden voyage on 11 June 1929 under the command of Captain Arthur Porter. The new ship quickly developed a reputation for high standards and punctuality. The 18 knot service speed allowed her to complete the 275 km journey within the designated nine hour crossing time regardless of the state of the tide at Liverpool. All three ships did, however, suffer from a significant vibration problem which was particularly felt in the steerage class quarters aft. Arrival at Liverpool was timetabled for 0700 hours, and a free bus service connected passengers with the main line railway termini in the city. This timing was preferred by many to the rather uncivilised 0500 hours transfer from ship to train which the railway steamers then undertook at Heysham.

In the 1930s, the **Ulster Prince** took time off to carry out several summer seasons of weekend cruises from Liverpool to the west coast of Scotland. The **Ulster Queen** was also initially used for these but the **Ulster Monarch** always stayed on service as she had a slightly lower deadweight and, therefore, marginally higher cargo capacity than her sisters. Typical destinations included Tobermory, Ballachulish, Fort William and Oban, or Arrochar, Bute and Oban, although no calls were specifically advertised other than 'turning at the north end of the Sound of Mull'. The **Ulster Prince** briefly grounded on Rathlin Island during her final cruise in 1939.

The vibration problem was tackled on the **Ulster Monarch** during an extensive overhaul in 1937. She received new propellers and the shaft plummer blocks were placed on rubber mats. The opportunity was also taken to combine the smoke room, the adjacent verandah café and the enclosed area of the Boat Deck to form one large room. Oddly, her two sisters were not altered.

*Early morning on the Mersey as the **Ulster Monarch** (1929) approaches Princes Lock on arrival from Belfast towards the end of her career. Note the open bulwarks on the Boat Deck.*

Even before the new ships had been properly evaluated on the Belfast service an order had been placed with Harland & Wolff for a fourth motor ship, this time for the City of Cork Steam Packet Company which was also now a part of the Coast Lines Group. Until 1926 their Cork to Fishguard direct passenger service had been maintained by a variety of vessels including the old faithful steamer **Classic**, originally named **Magic**, and previously relief steamer on the Belfast to Liverpool route. Although most of the vessels used were adequate for the service they were no match for the new steamers then being planned for the Railway service out of Rosslare. It was very much a case of a new ship to ensure the success of the Cork service for many years to come.

She was given the name **Innisfallen**, and the service was immediately marketed under the banner 'The Innisfallen Route'. There were three sailings a week in each direction. The **Innisfallen** left Fishguard on

Tuesday, Thursday and Saturday at about midnight, depending on the punctuality of the train from London, and arrived at her berth at Penrose Quay, in the centre of Cork, at 0900 hours the next morning. She returned from Cork on Mondays, Wednesdays and Fridays at 1800 hours and was due in Fishguard at 0300 hours during the night, with direct rail connections alongside for Cardiff and London.

The *Innisfallen* was not an exact copy of the Ulster sisters. The main difference was that her overall length was only 98 m although she was of the same breadth. Her gross tonnage was 3071. She had a reduced cabin capacity for saloon passengers compared with the Belfast boats, but the standard of her accommodation was equally high. Outwardly, the main difference was that A Deck was open both at the aft end of the superstructure and beneath the bridge, which, as was the custom of the day, was of varnished timber construction. The two funnels sported the distinctive white and black top of the Cork ships and she also carried an attractive thin white strake beneath the midships superstructure. In addition there was no accommodation on C and D Decks

The *Innisfallen* settled to her weekly routine without fuss and with precious little incident. In 1935 she was temporarily placed on the Belfast to Glasgow route of Burns & Laird in order to assess the feasibility of this class of ship on that busy service. Although her ownership was officially transferred to British & Irish Steam Packet Company in 1936, the *Innisfallen* stayed loyal to her design route until shortly after the outbreak of war, when she was moved away from the exposed southern corridor to serve on her owner's Liverpool to Dublin service. Registered in Cork, the *Innisfallen* retained neutrality as the war progressed, but this was a neutrality that did not guarantee immunity from falling bombs and mines. Leaving Liverpool on 20 December 1940, at the end of a particularly fierce air raid, she hit a mine and sank off New Brighton with the loss of two of her crew and two of the cattle drovers that were aboard that night. All the 143 passengers were brought ashore safely, but the ship was not recoverable; a sad and untimely end to the world's fourth fast motor passenger ferry.

Unhappily two of the three Ulster ships were also lost because of the war. The **Ulster Prince** was requisitioned by the Admiralty. She was present at St Nazaire, following the capitulation of France, when the liner *Lancastria* arrived off the port on 17 June 1940. Having already loaded about 5000 men, the liner was bombed and sunk, as aircraft strafed men in the oily water, which later caught fire. The **Ulster Prince** sailed to this horrific scene to assist, only to be ordered back into port. At dawn the next day, she was finally able to leave in an 8 knot convoy for Falmouth under Captain J Wilson, with a total of 2850 survivors, all choked with heavy oil, some also suffering burns.

Later in 1940 the **HMS Ulster Prince** was taken in hand at Ardrossan and converted to a troop carrier, her crew enjoying a well deserved leave. There then followed a period of escort work in the Mediterranean which included night runs along the Libyan coast to the garrison at Tobruk. During the evacuation of Greece following its surrender to the Germans in April 1941, when the **HMS Ulster Prince** was part of Operation Demon to evacuate the ANZAC troops, she went aground approaching Nauplia harbour and was subsequently abandoned, after lightening ship under repeated attack by enemy aircraft on 25 April. The crew retreated to the hills above the town, later to be taken off by the cruiser **HMS Orion** along with a rearguard team of Australian and New Zealand troops. It took four months before the men got home to the UK.

The **Ulster Queen** fared little better in the war. She initially remained on the Belfast to Liverpool crossing but was driven ashore at Maughold Head, near Ramsey Bay, in gale conditions on 28 February 1940. Her Captain that night was J Arbuckle. The 93 passengers were successfully transferred to the London, Midland & Scottish Railway's steamer **Duke of Lancaster** which lay 3 km off-shore. This was done with the ship's own boats over a five hour period, during worsening weather conditions. The crew were taken off by breeches buoy as the tide rose. The **Ulster Queen** was refloated four weeks later, after part of the sea bed, including a number of rock pinnacles, had been blasted away.

After a preliminary survey in Ramsey Bay, the **Ulster Queen** proceeded on to Belfast under Captain J Hawthorn, arriving at her destination some 30 days after she had left Liverpool. Under normal conditions, she would have been declared a constructive loss, but the war dictated her conversion for use as a landing ship (infantry), and she was later altered again to a fighter direction ship. When peace resumed she was laid up at Milford Haven, but in a state beyond economic restoration to her former self, and she later left for the breaker's yard.

The **Ulster Monarch** led a distinguished and varied career in the war. She was involved in nearly every European and African campaign, and seemed to lead almost a charmed life. Her war effort started early in September 1939, carrying members of the British Expeditionary Force to France out of Southampton and later Avonmouth, after which she returned briefly to Liverpool to Belfast ferry duties. By April of the following year she was involved in the Norwegian campaign, returning in time to help repatriate parts of the British

Expeditionary Force from Brest. She was then dispatched to Casablanca returning via Gibraltar and Madeira, and then on to the occupation of Iceland and the Faroes.

In October 1940 she became **HMS Ulster Monarch**, joining the Combined Operations Fleet under Admiral Sir Roger Keyes. However, immediate plans for her were altered, as she became a troop transport based at Gibraltar, principally serving West African ports. In April 1942 she survived an intense storm, rolling alarmingly (see Chapter 14), and with the Promenade Deck bulwarks awash, the engines actually stalled briefly with water in the fuel. Safely back in Liverpool, she was converted to a Landing Ship for use in the North African Campaign landing a contingent of Rangers at Arzeu. She later circumnavigated Africa to leave Suez with the SAS for Syracuse and Augusta as part of the Sicily invasion force. She then became part of the Malta, North Africa and Sicily supply chain, during which she received a bomb on the poop, setting fire to petrol drums and munitions. She was also involved in the invasion of Salerno and the D Day landings.

A pamphlet was published by the Ulster Imperial Line, as the Belfast Steamship Company then preferred to be known, in the immediate post-war years, accredited to the Chief Officer of the **Ulster Monarch** throughout most of her wartime career, T F Wrigley, OBE, which described the ship's wartime exploits. These included a torpedo that penetrated the hull without exploding, an aircraft carrier which exploded and disintegrated adjacent to the ship, and a bomb that pierced the deck before going overboard. The author concluded:

"Could there be any significance in the carved wooden monstrosity that surmounted the newel post at the head of the smokeroom companionway? Always jealously guarded against depredations of the souvenir hunter, its disappearance would have caused consternation indeed!"

The **Ulster Monarch** received a major and well deserved refit in 1946, which included the installation of refrigerated cargo space. The public rooms aboard the **Ulster Monarch** were reinstated and wood panelling, that had been damaged or stripped out during the war years, was replaced. From 1950, the livery was attractive shiny red funnels with black tops and the hull was again black but with a thin white strake and red boot topping. Her top hamper was reduced in consequence of sailing with light loads in the immediate post-war years. All three of the Ulster ships had been tender sea boats, and the **Ulster Monarch**, of lower deadweight than her former sisters, had the worst propensity to roll. Outwardly her two funnels were reduced in height, and the bulwarks on the Boat Deck were replaced by cutting large oval holes and the insertion of railings. Her main mast was replaced by a shorter mast. During the early 1950s the red boot topping was replaced by a dull but distinctive green colour.

Two ships were now adequate for the service, as access to Princes Dock at Liverpool was available at all but the lowest of tides from 1950 onwards. The new consort for the **Ulster Monarch** was the former British & Irish Steam Packet Company's **Leinster** (Chapter 5), which was renamed **Ulster Prince** and painted in the company colours. Although accommodation on the two ships was broadly similar it was always possible to identify one from another, as the wood panelling on the former **Leinster** was distinctly lighter in tone than that used in the **Ulster Monarch**.

Throughout the 1950s and much of the 1960s these two stalwarts maintained a reliable and comfortable service. Renowned for cleanliness, good service and pleasant well-ventilated cabin accommodation, they continued to provide a leisurely crossing with no urgency to disembark on arrival. The waiter service restaurant remained a feature to the end. However, at the close of the 1966 season it was decided not to put the two elderly vessels through their surveys.

Aboard for the last return crossing on 1 October was Mr C E Hulme, General Passenger Manager for Coast Lines, who recalled that, when the **Ulster Monarch** first took up duties in 1929, he was a junior clerk in the Passage Office. He said: "No other ship has the same character as the **Ulster Monarch**, she has always been my favourite". The **Ulster Monarch** was dispatched to Van Heyghen Frères' ship-breaking yard in Ghent, complete with her original pair of B & W style 4-stroke cycle diesels that had been built 38 years previously under licence in Belfast. On her last voyage to the shipbreakers, the engineers opened up the throttle for the last time as she sailed through the Irish Sea, still capable of a steady 18 knots

The four pioneer ships, three at Belfast and one at Cork, were demonstrably successful. Their commercial career through the 1930s was sufficient for the Coast Lines management to order nine further diesel ferries of what was to became the Coast Lines Standard Passenger Ferry (Chapters 5 and 11). The last of this line of magnificent vessels was only delivered in 1957. The influence that this standard design was to have on all cross-channel services, the world over, was considerable.

TABLE 1 Coast Lines *Ulster Monarch*-class of diesel ferries

	Year built	Lost or scrapped	Grt (as built)	Reg length	No. of passenger berths	Speed (knots)	Engines
Ulster Monarch	1929	1966	3735	109	419 saloon 100 steerage	18	2 x B & W type 10-cylinder four stroke cycle
Ulster Queen	1930	1950	3735	109	419 saloon 100 steerage	18	2 x B & W type 10-cylinder four stroke cycle
Ulster Prince	1930	1941	3735	109	419 saloon 100 steerage	18	2 x B & W type 10-cylinder four stroke cycle
Innisfallen	1930	1940	3071	98	200 saloon 100 steerage	18	2 x B & W type 10-cylinder four stroke cycle
Royal Scotsman	1936	1984	3244	100	225 saloon 110 steerage	17	2 x Harland & Wolf B & W type 8-cylinder two stroke cycle
Royal Ulsterman	1936	1973	3244	100	225 saloon 110 steerage	17	2 x Harland & Wolf B & W type 8-cylinder two stroke cycle
Leinster/Ulster Prince	1937	1967	4302	108	425 saloon 120 steerage	18	2 x Harland & Wolf B & W type 10-cylinder two stroke cycle
Munster	1938	1940	4302	108	425 saloon 120 steerage	18	2 x Harland & Wolf B & W type 10-cylinder two stroke cycle
Leinster	1948	1987	4115	105	225 first class 107 third class	17	2 x Harland & Wolf B & W type 10-cylinder two stroke cycle
Munster	1948	2000	4088	105	225 first class 107 third class	17	2 x Harland & Wolf B & W type 10-cylinder two stroke cycle
Innisfallen*	1948	1985	3705	100	200 first class 100 third class	17	2 x Sulzer 12TS48 12-cylinder two stroke cycle
Irish Coast	1951	1989	3813	98	242 first class 146 third class	17	2 x Harland & Wolf B & W type 10-cylinder two stroke cycle
Scottish Coast	1957	2002	3817	98	246 first class 144 second class+	17	2 x Harland & Wolf B & W type 10-cylinder two stroke cycle

* Built by William Denny at Dumbarton; all others built by Harland & Wolff at Belfast

+ Third class was retitled second class from 1956, in line with British Railways

THE COAST LINES SEAWAY

The name The Coast Line came into being in April 1917, having been adopted in advertisements of Powell, Bacon and Hough Lines, itself formed in 1913 by amalgamation of three coastal shipping companies. From the outset, Coast Lines adopted the black funnel with its distinctive white chevron and later began to name its vessels with the well known "Coast" nomenclature. The Chairman of Powell, Bacon and Hough Lines was Alfred Read, a dynamic young man. In the five years following the amalgamation in 1913, Read bought a Liverpool cartage company, become a member of the Irish Railway Clearing House (both shrewd moves for an independent company unable to make inroads with the English railway companies) and staked an investment in the British & Irish Steam Packet Company. So influential had the company become in the coasting trades that it came to the attention of the mighty Royal Mail Group. The Royal Mail Group was at that time interested in acquiring a coastal feeder system for its own many and diverse deep sea liner services, and was able to buy Coast Lines for £0.8 million. With the financial might of the Royal Mail Group, Coast Lines set about acquiring additional companies to strengthen its position in the coastal liner trades.

The Belfast Steamship Company was one of its first conquests along with the British and Irish Steam Packet Company, and this at a time of restricted sailings due to a down turn in trade caused by unrest in Ireland and the coal strike. Shortly afterwards the interests of G & J Burns and the Laird line were brought together as Burns and Laird within the Coast Line umbrella. Although the Coast Line partners flourished in the 1920s, the parent Royal Mail Line Group, under Lord Kylsant, was encountering increasing financial difficulties. A number of measures were taken within Coast Lines to insulate it from the inevitable downfall of the parent company, ironically aided by the intransigence of Lord Kylsant to refinance the company in 1922. The fall of both Lord Kylsant and the Royal Mail Group finally occurred in 1931. Coast Lines and its associate company were now sufficiently independent to ride out the storm, and were able to buy themselves out of the Royal Mail Group altogether in 1936.

The subsequent history of the group is legion; Coast Lines being the one major independent sea carrier in steadfast competition with the railways. Coast Lines Limited controlled amongst others: Belfast Steamship Company Limited; British & Irish Steam Packet Limited; Burns & Laird Lines Limited; Belfast, Mersey and Manchester Steamship Company; British Channel Islands Shipping Company Limited and Island Shipping Company Limited; Tyne-Tees Steam Shipping Company Limited and Aberdeen Steam Navigation Company Limited; Queenships Limited; A Coker & Company Limited; Coast Lines Africa (Pty) Limited; Zillah Shipping Company Limited; William Sloan & Company Limited; and jointly with the London, Midland & Scottish Railway, David MacBrayne Limited. It had also incorporated such well known names as M Langlands & Sons in 1919, and Robert Gilchrist & Company in 1943. In addition, Coast Lines' own fleet of distinctively named and liveried coasters was to be a common feature at British ports until the rationalisation of the coasting trade with the onset of containerisation and roll-on traffic.

Few major passenger units were adorned in the parent company colours and of the big diesel ferries, only the **Irish Coast** (Chapter 11) was to carry the white chevron throughout her career. In 1961, Coast Lines bought the North of Scotland, Orkney and Shetland Shipping Company Limited for a mere £1.1 million. The former Scottish company was in trouble for having over committed itself to conventional tonnage (much as Coast Lines itself had also done until that time) rather than invest in container and roll-on roll-off equipment. Tyne-Tees Steam Shipping was a founder member of North Sea Ferries in 1965, along with P&O. This partnership eventually led to the mighty P&O organisation buying the whole of Coast Lines for £5.6 million in 1971. The white chevron on a black funnel was seen no more, and the surviving ships of the subsidiaries, Belfast Steamship Company and Burns & Laird Lines, were soon disguised with their new corporate identity.

Today, the ships of P&O continue the passenger and cargo trade once maintained by the diesel ferries of the Coast Lines seaway on the Irish Sea, although now registered overseas.

CHAPTER 4

THE MACBRAYNE LOCHS

In 1928 David MacBrayne Limited was reconstituted under the joint ownership of the London, Midland & Scottish Railway and Coast Lines. Coast Lines were still in an expansive mood at this time, but part of the terms of the constitution of the new company was an obligation to build four new ships within two years. The first of these was the **Lochness**, a modest conventional steamer, albeit oil fired, designed to maintain the Mallaig, Kyle and Stornoway mail service at a service speed of 14 knots. The remaining three vessels were all diesel driven, and in addition the company built and commissioned a diesel driven cargo vessel, the **Lochshiel**, although she was not part of the reconstitution deal. The Coast Lines influence is obvious. Given the success of the four Harland & Wolff cross channel ships described in Chapter 3, this same design and engineering policy clearly influenced the MacBrayne directors.

The **Lochshiel** was equipped with a single direct reversing single acting 6-cylinder two stroke Gardner Denver engine which could generate 225 kW at 290 revolutions per minute. The cylinder bores were 318 mm and the stroke was 380 mm. The ship also had a small oil fired auxiliary boiler to power cargo winches and capstans. She was found to be a most economical unit, not least because the main engine could be shut down the minute she came alongside. Her service speed on the west coast cargo routes out of Glasgow was about 9 knots.

Of the three remaining passenger ships built as part of the reconstitution deal, two were identical sisters with direct-drive diesel engines, the **Lochearn** and **Lochmor**, and the last had her diesels coupled to generators to provide the first diesel-electric drive coastal passenger ship in the world. This was the **Lochfyne**. All three were commissioned with grey hulls but reverted to traditional black early in their careers.

The **Lochearn** and **Lochmor** were identical twins. They were built by Ardrossan Dockyard Limited, part of the Royal Mail Group of which Coast Lines was then a part. They were launched respectively on 29 April and 15 May 1930. Viewed from the bows they looked businesslike and not unattractive. Abeam and from the stern, their solid central superstructure and almost vertical single funnel, coupled with their plump and ungainly cruiser sterns and grey hulls, pursuaded Duckworth and Langmuir (see reference section) to liken them to a pair of wooden models in a toyshop window. The machinery was a double version of that installed in the cargo boat **Lochshiel,** i.e. twin 6-cylinder engines and twin direct-drive screws in each ship. The actual design speed for the ships was over 12 knots, but in practice they could only manage just over 9 knots. Their lack of power was summed up by one of their masters: "They canna get oot their ain road!". Another disadvantage was that the machinery was extremely noisy and there was no escape for passengers from the constant rattle of the engines and the thumping of the exhaust discharge.

The **Lochearn** (1930) as built with grey hull and tall funnel, along with the **Mountaineer** (1910) alongside Oban's North Pier in June 1931.

(Alistair Deayton collection)

The **Lochearn** (1930) in Loch Scavaig.
(Alistair Deayton)

On the plus side, the pair were very well appointed but there was little wasted space, with accommodation for 400 passengers in ships of only 542 tons gross. Cabin accommodation was provided in single and double cabins for first class passengers only. The cabins were reported to be comfortable, and each had a sink with hot and cold running water. The first class public rooms featured a lounge and a smoke room bar, and the dining room had numerous separate small tables, with waiter silver service for each meal. The third class public rooms were situated aft, but both classes had access to covered deck space. Both ships had a single hold forward and this was served by an electric winch and derrick.

During the 1930s, the **Lochearn** was based at Oban, on the Barra, South Uist, Coll and Tiree Islands Mail Service, whilst the **Lochmor** maintained the Mallaig and Kyle run to South Uist, North Uist and Harris, calling also at Eigg and Rum.

The final ship of the quartet was even more radical. This was the first diesel-electric drive coastal passenger ship, the **Lochfyne**. The electric coupling was intended to overcome the difficulties of manoeuvring off coastal piers and jetties with strong currents, given only coarse control over the twin screws from the direct-reversing diesels then available.

The **Lochfyne** was built by William Denny of Dumbarton, an innovation in itself as this was the first MacBrayne ship ever to be ordered from that yard. Her total cost was £60,950. She was launched on 20 March 1931 and was handed over to her owners on 28 May, two months later. Outwardly she had a slightly raked stem, a pleasing cruiser stern and twin funnels, the forward one being a dummy.

The novel power units comprised two Metropolitan Vickers 500 kW electric motors supplied by 520 volt direct current and capable of a full load speed of 433 revolutions per minute. The motors were coupled directly to the propellers. The main generators were each rated at 520 kW and were driven by twin 5-cylinder Davey-Paxman in-line, four stroke single acting diesels with an output of 750 kW at 330 revolutions per minute. The cylinder bore was 403 mm and the stroke 508 mm. The diesels were turbocharged by an exhaust gas turbine connected to a single stage blower. Known as the Buchi system the fan supercharged the engine by blowing air into the explosive cycle at a faster rate than it could unaided. Auxiliary generators, which were driven by the main engines in tandem with the main generator units, supplied 230 volt direct current for lighting, heating, cooking and capstan operation and there was a Gardner diesel generator for use when the main engines were shut down.

The main switch-gear was located at a control platform in sight of both the diesel engine starting gear and the electrical controls. At the throw of a single switch, control could be given directly to the bridge, where a normal telegraph interpreted instructions regarding motor speed and direction by selecting the voltage and current supplied to the motors. The balance between propulsion motor speed and generator field regulators was controlled only from the engine room. Trials saw the ship successfully satisfy her contract speed of 16 knots, and at 0.25 kg/kW specific fuel consumption her daily fuel costs amounted to about £3 10 shillings, half that of a conventional vessel at that time.

The **Lochfyne** (1931) at East Loch Tarbert in July 1969. The vessel suffered from a serious vibration problem. Described more as a shimmering than a rattle, it was most intense when the main engines were running and the ship was stopped rather than under way. How apt it was that 'Dumbarton Drums are Beating' had been played by the pipers at her launching!

Although the **Lochfyne**'s vibration is mentioned in a variety of contemporary texts – for example 'she shimmied like an oriental belly dancer', it may be that expectations were higher in the 1930s, when the silence of the steam turbine engine set the standard, than they are today. One little irony was the incorporation of waist high observation hatches to the engine room, which maintained the age old tradition of passengers 'going down to see the engines'. However, the ear splitting roar emerging from the void and the throbbing engine casings below were a contrast to the old vision of sliding cranks and connecting rods and the smell of hot oil.

The **Lochfyne** was also unique in that she offered only passenger accommodation. There was no provision for the carriage of cargo other than passengers' baggage (which from time to time might include the odd animal on its way inbound to market or outbound to improve the blood line of the island stock). The passenger accommodation was adaptable and enabled her to operate as a one class day ship in summer on the Oban to Staffa and Iona service, and later also the Fort William excursions, whereas she became a two class day ship in winter for the Ardrishaig mail service on the Clyde. There was no cabin accommodation. However, with a gross tonnage of only 748, her licensed passenger complement of 1200 is still remarkable (although uncomfortable with a full load on board). The accommodation was, nonetheless, strikingly up to date and was designed around the theme of purpose, comfort and ease of maintenance. However, her Promenade Deck suffered from obstructions such as ventilators, and passengers were obliged to watch where they walked as they admired the passing views.

All went well for the **Lochfyne** until 25 July 1939. With her main engines running slowly whilst alongside at Oban the starboard diesel engine suddenly exploded. An eye witness, Captain Mackinnon's son, who was present in the engine room, reported:

"First of all there was a terrific noise like cars back-firing, followed by metal being flung and scattered all over the engine room, breaking the gauge glasses and mangling the iron ladders leading down from the Main Deck. Clouds of dense black smoke then filled the engine room."

The ship returned to Greenock on her remaining engine, but with the single generator coupled to both motors. Inspection revealed that the catastrophic failure of the engine was caused by a fractured bottom end bolt in the Number 1 Cylinder. Replacement parts and repairs took eight months and the **Lochfyne** returned to service in March 1940. For the full duration of the war she served on the Ardrishaig Mail Route from Wemyss Bay, which was below the safety of the Cloch-Dunoon anti-submarine boom.

Both the **Lochearn** and the **Lochmor** happily led uneventful lives throughout the war, and all three ships survived unscathed when hostilities ceased. However, their original engines were all becoming unreliable, and a programme of re-engining began as soon as suitable machinery became available. The first to be dealt with was the **Lochearn**, which returned to her builders in 1948 to receive a pair of Paxman-Ricardo V12 diesels, each with twelve cylinders arranged in a V configuration, and each providing 225 kW at 1000 revolutions per minute. Each cylinder had a bore of 178 mm and a modest stroke of 195 mm. The engines had originally been destined for fitting in Landing Craft (Tanks), and their incredible noise had to be inhibited by portable acoustic hoods. Although the original direct-drive propellers and shafts were retained, Modern Wheel Drive Limited SLM-type reverse/reduction gearing was coupled with the crank shaft, which was now situated some 0.4 m above the propeller shaft. The **Lochearn** returned to service in July, with the **Lochmor** going back to Ardrossan that Autumn to receive the same treatment. She, in turn, emerged with her new machinery in June 1949. Each ship now retained a third engine ashore for overhaul, in order to reduce down time in the event of engine failure.

With their new geared machinery, the two ships could at last attain their original design speed and, with the engines producing a full 450 kW, they could maintain a service speed just in excess of 11.5 knots. The noise of the engines in the passenger accommodation was an improvement on pre-war days, although it was never possible to get completely away from the roar of the engines. Both ships also sported a shorter and slightly dumpier aluminium funnel.

They returned to their civilian routines until the **Lochearn** was displaced from the Oban Islands mail service by new building (the **Claymore**) in 1955 (see Chapter 11), and the **Lochmor** was displaced by a new breed of side loading car ferry (the **Hebrides**) in 1964 (see Chapter 12). The **Lochearn** then maintained the Sound of Mull service between 1955 and 1964. Then the twins actually worked together briefly as car ferries on the Mull service (crane on, crane off!), until both were sold at the end of the summer season for further service in the Mediterranean, this time displaced by the new car ferry **Clansman**. The elderly motor ferries survived in the Greek islands until 1969, although the **Lochearn** saw additional service under another new owner which lasted into the early 1980s.

After yet another major mechanical failure, the *Lochfyne* received her new engines in the spring of 1953. She was given a pair of British Polar type K44M 4-cylinder two stroke engines. The cylinders on these engines had a bore of 331 mm and a stroke of 571 mm. Individually the new engines developed 600 kW at 330 revolutions per minute, and on trials she managed just under 17 knots. The vibrations, characteristic of her first set of engines, were as bad as ever and strengthening bars had to be added to the bedplates. In time the engine vibration lessened, and towards the end of her career it had become less intrusive. Ian Ramsey of The Institution of Engineers and Shipbuilding in Scotland writes:

"I also served on this ship, and she suffered from horrendous vibration and airborne noise. The vibration was so bad that the compass bowl in the binnacle in the wheelhouse was mounted on damping springs as were the clock and the barometer, and the foremast continually whipped back and forth like a fishing rod about to cast a fly. The noise was not helped by the fact that the engine room had viewing windows along the length of the Main Deck and many were open for ventilation which resulted in the whole midship area of the ship being subjected to a deafening roar."

With her new engines she maintained broadly the same schedule as before. On the retirement of the elderly *Saint Columba* from the summer Ardrishaig service in 1958, the *Lochfyne* took sole charge of this prestigious route all year round. Minor alteration at that time included the removal of the ship's centre staircase on the Main Deck and the installation of two separate stairs, one to port and one to starboard. This allowed a new extension of the Shade Deck aft.

Unhappily, the *Lochfyne* suffered another mechanical mishap. On 4 October 1965 she was on route to Tarbert from Rothesay when a piece of debris became lodged in the port main generator cooling trunking and got trapped in the generator. A small fire was quickly extinguished and the ship was able to return via Tarbert to Greenock under her own power using the starboard set only. The port generator had to be completely rewound, and the starboard one stripped and cleaned, as fire extinguisher fluid had penetrated the windings. The armature of the port generator created a problem as the large number of soft iron laminates pressed into the core had been varnished on assembly to prevent eddy currents from developing. The varnish had been damaged in the fire and nobody knew what thickness or what type of varnish should be applied. Help was at hand when an elderly craftsman, who had worked on the generators in 1929 was located to advise on the reconstruction. The ship was out of commission for a total of seven months.

The *Lochfyne* made her last return trip to Ardrishaig on 30 September 1969. This was the result of the acquisition of David MacBrayne and the Caledonian Steam Packet Company by the Scottish Transport Group, who promptly closed the service. She was sold early in 1970, ostensibly for demolition, but was moved to Faslane on the Gareloch to act as an electrical generating plant, and was resold in 1972 to Scottish & Newcastle Breweries, for use as a floating pub. Alas, this last scheme came to nothing, and she was towed to Dalmuir in March 1974 for breaking up.

The obvious success of diesel-electric propulsion in the MacBrayne fleet led to an order for a second ship much along the lines of the *Lochfyne*. This was the *Lochnevis*, and she was launched from Dumbarton on 15 May 1934 at the height of the Great Depression. She was built almost solely by apprentices under the direction of Head Foremen, for the sum of £45,999. There were a number of significant differences between the two ships, not least that the *Lochnevis* had a shorter hull form and that she had a single hold forward. Her machinery was subtly different as well, in that the generating equipment was provided by General Electric. Otherwise her twin 6-cylinder four stroke Davey-Paxman engines (cylinder bore of 330 mm and stroke of 406 mm) each developed 460 kW at 400 revolutions per minute, which in turn generated 500 volt direct current, with a power of up to 420 kW each. The motors were placed well aft of the generating room, being separated by the Lower Deck first class smoking room and bar. At 400 revolutions per minute, the motors each produced 395 kW of power and drove the ship at just under 15 knots. Control of the motors was directly from the bridge or it could be transferred to the engine room control platform if desired.

The problem of vibration was largely overcome aboard the *Lochnevis*. This was accomplished by mounting the bed plates for the two diesel engines on a series of damping springs which prevented the vibration from penetrating the hull (much as Manchester's new Bridgwater Hall sits on huge springs in order to isolate this concert hall from the rumble of passing traffic). As her engine room was totally enclosed, the only noise heard was when an engine room door was opened. However, the cluttered Promenade Deck was as before, and the bridge platform was raised by just over a metre above this deck level to accommodate the bridge control contactor gear, just as it was on the *Lochfyne*.

The *Lochnevis* was designed specifically for the Mallaig, Kyle and Portree service. During the summer she also undertook cruises to the Gairloch and Loch Torridon from Portree, and from Mallaig to Loch Scavaig. The accommodation was again of a high standard, with public rooms originally laid out in two classes, but as a day ship there was no cabin accommodation. The war years saw her on ferry duties on the Clyde until she was requisitioned as a minelayer, to become **HMS Lochnevis** until June 1944, when she again took up ferry duties out of Wemyss Bay.

She too received a new set of engines, this time in March 1957. These were manufactured in Ashton-under-Lyne by National Gas and Oil Engine Company, and produced 1190 kW power. They were twin 6-cylinder four stroke single acting diesel engines with a cylinder bore of 305 mm and a stroke of 381 mm. The new engines were coupled to the same generating sets and motors. Once back in service, the **Lochnevis** soon left the Portree run, as traffic then allowed smaller vessels to maintain this service. Oban became her new home, and she became responsible for a variety of rosters including Fort William, a weekly run down to Islay and excursions. The ship was finally retired at the end of the 1969 season, and sold shortly afterwards for demolition in Holland.

*The **Lochnevis** (1934) leaving Oban in August 1967.*

These pioneer diesel and diesel-electric vessels were followed by a number of diesel driven ships in the MacBrayne fleet of similar overall design. However, these early vessels all led highly successful careers, and came from a design era in which the diesel was favoured (shut down main engines at the end of the day, start up the next morning), but in which the later sophistication in engine control had not yet been developed. All four of them, the diesel twins **Lochmor** and **Lochearn** and the two diesel-electric Lochs, deserve their place in maritime history as a significant group of vessels in the introduction of diesel propulsion in short-sea passenger transport.

The diesel electric coupling was also adopted for the short Govan ferry crossing on the upper Clyde in the **Vehicular Ferryboat No 4**, built by Ferguson Brothers in 1938. She was equipped with twin 6-cylinder Davey-Paxman engines driving 160 kW generators and GEC motors. She closed the Govan crossing in 1966 and then the Finnieston crossing in 1967 and was later used for a short time as a drilling platform. During the war she assisted fire fighters with the blazing cruiser **HMS Sussex**, but her main claim to fame was her vehicle deck which could be raised according to the state of the tide to facilitate loading and unloading.

In 1939, a further MacBrayne ship, the **Lochiel**, was completed for the West Loch Tarbert to Islay route. The **Lochiel** was equipped with two 8-cylinder Paxman-Ricardo Comet Head engines, each providing 330 kW at 400 revolutions per minute, connected to reversing reduction gears and twin shafts. The engines were of the totally enclosed monobloc forced lubrication type. The design speed was 12 knots, although a comfortable 14 knots was attained on trials. This arrangement made maximum use of the relatively light weight medium speed engines rather than the heavier and slower direct reversing engines which were then in more common use. An auxiliary Paxman-Ricardo engine drove a 40 kW generator to provide 220 volts and a second engine powered the air compressor.

Launched from Denny's yard on 4 April 1939, the **Lochiel** was quickly placed in service. Almost vibration free, the earlier experience had been invested in flexible engine mountings to reduce both noise and vibration. Built with two class accommodation, first class to starboard, third class to port, the respective dining saloons and smoke rooms were on the Main Deck with the lounges, purser's office and ticket office on the Promenade Deck. As with the earlier ships, the bridge was raised above the Boat Deck to rail level, preventing passengers from seeing forward of the bridge, but affording the navigating officer excellent all round vision. In common with the **Lochnevis**, there was a single hold forward, served by a derrick on the single steel pole mast.

The **Lochiel** spent most of her career on her design route, and remained on station during the war. The passage up West Loch Tarbert was always a slow and purposeful glide through waters, which turn from green at the seaward end to thick peaty brown, as the loch narrows and twists between high ground on either side. Not surprisingly the **Lochiel** eventually fell foul of the obstructions which lay within the waters of the loch, partially sinking on striking rocks on 8 October 1960. Repaired and back in service by the following March, she was finally withdrawn in 1970. She became the **Norwest Laird** under the ownership of Norwest Shipping and was used on a summer excursion service from Fleetwood to the Isle of Man. In this guise, she only completed fourteen round trips, as her passenger certificate required her to hug the Cumbrian coast, making the passage time about 6 hours. There was also a number of engine failures, now that she was divorced from her MacBrayne engineers. She later adopted a static role at Bristol where she was eventually broken up in 1995.

The **Lochiel** (1939) setting off down West Loch Tarbert at low tide in July 1969.

Table 2 The MacBrayne-class of early diesel and diesel-electric ferries

	Year built	Last year in active service	Grt (as built)	No. of pax	Speed (knots)	Original engines	Power (kW)
Lochearn	1930	1983	542	400	9	2 x 6-cylinder Gardner Denver [1]	450
Lochmor	1930	1969	542	400	9	2 x 6-cylinder Gardner Denver [2]	450
Lochfyne	1930	1974	748	1200	16	2 x 5-cylinder Davey-Paxman [3] coupled to Metropolitan Vickers generators and 500 kW motors	750
Lochnevis	1930	1969	568	670	15	2 x 6-cylinder four-stroke cycle Davey-Paxman [4] coupled to General Electric generators and 790 kW motors	920
Lochiel	1939	1970	580	656	14	2 x 8-cylinder four-stroke cycle Paxman-Ricardo 'Comet Head' vertical diesels coupled to reverse reduction gearbox	660
Loch Seaforth	1947	1973	1089	500	14	2 x 6-cylinder Sulzer two-stroke diesel engines	1125
Claymore	1955	1976	1024	494	12	2 x 8-cylinder Sulzer two-stroke diesel engines	975

Notes

1 Re-engined in 1948
2 Re-engined in 1949
3 Re-engined in 1953
4 Re-engined in 1957

THE PAXMAN RICARDO V12 AND V16 ENGINES

The V12 engine was conceived from a suggestion by General A E Davidson of the Royal Arsenal in Woolwich to Ted Paxman. The proposal was for a power unit for large tanks, and a prototype was in service at the Army and Navy Stores power station in 1938. However, the tank idea was pursued no further at that time. The engine was designed around a 60º V, with the exhausts on the outside of the engine and with a Ricardo Comet combustion system. Maintenance was straight forward; the pistons could be removed through the crankcase doors. The maximum output per cylinder was 46 kW, a considerable advance over other small pre-war engines. The engine was popular for power generation and pumping. Its first marine application was on the motor torpedo boat **HMS Tarret**. With an unarmed displacement of 115 tons, the boat achieved 30 knots on trials. The exhaust manifolds were uncooled on this early version and glowed red hot at full power! Nevertheless, the boat did not go into production, and other ideas, again for tanks and a proposal for giant excavators to dig the Maginot Line, came and went. In the meantime orders for nearly 400 engines were fulfilled, later to be put into Tank Landing Craft. Eventually some 5000 engines were made, each in three parts, with the crankcase only meeting the two cylinder blocks at Paxman's Colchester works, with manufacture of the three individual pieces elsewhere (final assembly took one woman and a boy 60 hours to complete). The engine was used to power seven out of an order of eight gunboats for Turkey, and these were taken over by the Navy before completion in 1940. These boats had three V16 engines which had water cooled manifolds of cupro-nickel, and water cooled silencers. The main problems occurred through the crankshaft, due to torsional oscillation at high speed, but this was soon resolved. Five of the boats were converted in 1943 to fast merchant ships with a 45 ton payload, incorporating a small hold forward and another aft of the engine room. Their service speed was 23 knots. With Ellerman's Wilson Line officers and Hull trawlermen for crew they were used to run ball bearings from SKF in Sweden to the Humber. Nine successful round trips were completed in the five dark winter months, but many trips were aborted due to weather or mechanical failure, and one boat was captured by the Germans. Subsequent summer operations were less successful. This same design of engine was available in profusion in post-war years and it was the V12 type engines which were used for the re-engining of the **Lochearn** and **Lochmor**, although the **Lochinvar** was fitted with two 6-cylinder in-line engines (see Chapter 2). Although the engines were not intended for very high speed operation (coupled in any case to reduction/reverse gearing on the MacBrayne ships), the pedigree of the engines bore no relationship to this ultimate civilian use. This same engine design was later developed further and became the forerunner of the V range of small marine engines which were popular in the 1980s.

CHAPTER 5

IRISH SEA FERRIES AND THE INTERNATIONAL CONTEXT

During the 1930s, diesel engines were used by continental ship-owners to power new ferries on fast services between Dover and Ostend, Harwich and the Hook of Holland, Harwich and Esbjerg and Newcastle and Bergen. In addition, two second hand passenger and cargo vessels were bought for use on a service between London and Rotterdam. Diesel-engined ferries for the British registry were confined to four more of the so called Coast Lines' standard ships and one innovative roll-on roll-off ferry built to the order of the London, Midland & Scottish Railway. All the British ships were for use on the Irish Sea.

At the start of war, in September 1939, there were nine fast British-flagged diesel ferries, and another seven under continental ownership serving British ports. There were also the two London to Rotterdam cargo/passenger ships. In addition, a number of relatively small and slow diesel driven cargo ships had been built for coastal liner traffic, typically capable of carrying about twelve passengers. These included ships in the Coast Lines' fleet (Chapter 9) and four Danish ferries used on the Harwich to Esbjerg service.

The first building to follow the **Ulster Monarch**-class ferries was the Bergen Steamship Company's **Venus** (5407 gross tons). She was completed at Elsinore in 1931, and was given twin Burmeister & Wain 10-cylinder four stroke cycle engines, which gave her a speed of 20 knots. She was built following the success of the famous cruise yacht **Stella Polaris**, which had been completed in 1927 with similar 8-cylinder engines. The **Venus** was so successful that a second larger and faster ship, the **Vega** (with an impressive 7287 gross tons), was completed in 1938. The latter ship was sadly lost in the war, but the **Venus** survived. She was taken over by the German occupying forces in Norway, and was found on the bottom of Hamburg harbour in 1945. Extensively reconditioned, the **Venus** was returned to service in the North Sea until withdrawn in 1967.

The next group of fast diesel ferries were built to the order of the Belgian Marine Administration. Originally planned as the world's fastest steam turbine ferries, in an attempt to defeat the industrial crisis of the early 1930s, the technical advisor to the Administration persuaded them to think again. The arguments that compact engine room and greater payload of passengers, equal power ahead and astern, capability to shut down main engines in port, economy of operation and the overall increasing reliability and cleanliness of diesel power eventually won the day. Sadly, the proponent of the argument, Monsieur Grimard, died a young man shortly after his vision was commissioned.

The first of the Belgian ships was the **Prince Baudouin** (3050 tons gross), completed at the John Cockerill Société Anonyme of Hoboken near Antwerp in 1934 for the day passenger only service between Dover and Ostend. Repeat orders produced the **Prins Albert** in 1937 and the **Prince Phillippe** in 1939. (The latter escaped from her builders at the onset of the German invasion with only one engine, later to be completed in England.)

*The **Prins Albert** (1937) coming through the western entrance to Dover harbour stern first.*

(Ferry Publications)

The three ships had a raked stem and cruiser stern, a single squat perpendicular funnel and two rakeless masts giving them a modern and purposeful appearance. Each had twin high speed Sulzer 12-cylinder two stroke cycle direct-reversing engines, and were capable of maintaining a service speed of 22.5 knots at 250 revolutions per minute, and each attained over 25 knots on trials with a engine output of 570 kW. When completed, the **Prince Baudouin** was the fastest diesel vessel to date. She commenced service on 12 August 1934, and was extremely well received by the public. The accommodation was decorated in the Art Nouveau/Odean style and was distributed across five decks, with first class accommodation forward and second class aft. There was even a ladies' boudoir situated on C Deck.

After three months service, the **Prince Baudouin** was temporarily taken out of service to inspect the engines.. Hairline cracks in the nickel piston heads were rectified by using steel replacements. However, design fears of engine vibration had proved totally unfounded. The new ship then became the largest ever to travel up the canal to Brussels (a trip which required over 300 engine manoeuvres!) – there to be put on show to the public after being inspected by the King, and receiving 10,000 visitors a day. The youngest member of the trio was lost early in the war when she collided with the **Empire Wave** off the west coast of Scotland. The other two had a busy and varied war service, resuming civilian duties on release from the Admiralty in 1946. Both ships maintained a career of 30 years, the **Prince Baudouin** being withdrawn in 1964, the **Prins Albert** in 1969.

The next set of diesel ferries were for the British registry. They were the **Royal Ulsterman** and **Royal Scotsman** for Burns & Laird, and the **Leinster** and **Munster** for the British & Irish Steam Packet Company. It is interesting to again pick up the Coast Lines' history in order to appreciate the reasoning behind the orders for the first pair of these ships.

Virtually the last thing that G & J Burns had done before joining the Coast Lines Group was to give up their express summer only daylight service between Belfast and Ardrossan. This happened at the end of the 1919 season when the fast turbine steamer **Viper**, which dated from 1906, was put up for sale, and shortly afterwards became the Isle of Man Steam Packet Company's **Snaefell**. The withdrawal from the route reflected the increasingly unsettled situation in Ireland at that time. The 1920 season saw the slower **Graphic** of the Belfast Steamship Company maintain the route, Coast Lines now having a vested interest, as they had acquired the Ardrossan Harbour Company (as well as the Ardrossan Drydock and Shipbuilding Company). The **Graphic** was not a success and the service was not repeated in 1921.

The Ardrossan day route was revived in 1926, and was maintained by a variety of vessels. Eventually the turbine steamer **Riviera**, built in 1911 for the South Eastern & Chatham Railway, was bought for this service, renamed **Lairds Isle** and placed under the Burns & Laird Line flag. The overnight Belfast to Ardrossan service was maintained throughout and offered through rail connections with Dublin and Glasgow. This service was maintained by the elderly and somewhat dilapidated **Lairdsgrove** and **Lairdsrock**, and was hardly competition against the new turbine steamer **Princess Margaret**, which had started on the Stranraer to Larne route in 1931. This competition from the London, Midland & Scottish Railway concentrated the minds of the Coast Lines' board, who took the decision in 1935 to re-equip its overnight Belfast to Glasgow service.

This decision led to the order for the next generation of diesel driven Coast Lines' standard ferries, the **Royal Ulsterman** and the **Royal Scotsman**. Three quarters of the building costs for the pair, some £292 000 was borrowed from the Midland Bank, with a financial guarantee from the Ministry of Finance for Northern Ireland. Although the proposed ships were to be a little smaller than the **Ulster Monarch**-class they would be much bigger than anything used previously on the Glasgow service.

The other significant difference from the earlier ships is that the new pair was equipped with the more efficient two stroke cycle engine. The engines were Harland & Wolff B&W type, built by Harland under licence from Burmeister & Wain, each with 16 cylinders of 50 mm bore and 90 mm stroke. The twin engines provided a nominal power of 810 kW, which provided the ships with a service speed of 18 knots. In an attempt to overcome the vibration problems encountered in the earlier ships, the twin propellers were set very wide and projected outside the beam of the vessel. The ships were found to be much less prone to vibration than the Belfast – Liverpool trio, but the widely spaced propellers prevented them from ever deputising on that service, as they were too wide to enter Princes Dock at Liverpool.

The **Royal Ulsterman** was launched at Belfast on 10 March 1936, and her sister followed her into the water the next day. They each had a pleasingly raked stem and a single oval shaped funnel. The **Royal Scotsman** was ready to take an invited party to Fort William on 1 June, and both ships began the new service on the 15 June. The two sisters differed only in the one being registered in Belfast with a shamrock weather vane on her mainmast and the other registered in Glasgow with a thistle at the foremast. The saloon passengers were accommodated in single cabins and two-berth cabins on A and B Decks and cabins de luxe with private baths which were all situated on the Promenade Deck. There was no accommodation below in the 'tween decks, as there was on the Ulster ships. This area was reserved for cattle, although in the height of the summer season the 'tween deck space could be converted for third class use. Saloon class public rooms included a restaurant on B Deck, a lounge on A Deck and a smoke room situated forward of the de-luxe cabin accommodation on the Promenade Deck. The third class accommodation was a great improvement on that to be found on the Ulster-class with two berth cabins, and a restaurant, smoke room and a so called general room.

The ships were equipped with direction finding equipment, echo depth sounders and a bow rudder to help manoeuvrability whilst going astern. The only other innovation was that the traditional red with black top funnel carried a dusty blue band between the red and the black. This was not a popular move but it remained with the Burns & Laird ships to the end (it apparently had to do with the artistic flair of the Company Chairman's wife!).

The two ships proved highly successful on their design route and even managed to fit in occasional day returns between Belfast and Ardrossan on certain summer Saturdays. Both ships were employed on trooping duties during the war years, and were together during the Norwegian campaign and the later evacuation of St Nazaire in 1940, and during 1942 and 1943 they were again together for the North Africa and Italy landings. The ships were returned to their owners in time for the full North Channel service to be resumed for the winter of 1946/47. With the exception of war service, and occasional day trips to Ardrossan, they only ever deviated from the Glasgow route on very rare occasions with a couple of football specials to Dublin.

*The **Royal Ulsterman** (1936) arriving at Glasgow in July 1967*

The two Royal stalwarts maintained the overnight connection between the two cities until 1967. The **Royal Scotsman** completed her last commercial voyage in September and was immediately sold to the cult following known as Scientology. Renamed the **Royal Scotman** and later the **Apollo**, she was described in the *Sunday Times* the following year as "a rusting and singularly grubby ex-Irish Sea ferry". She was later sold for static use in Texas, then for use as a salvage ship. Whilst being converted for this role and carrying the new name **Arctic Star**, she was hit by a train (!) and, following a long legal wrangle, was scrapped in 1984 as she lay.

The **Royal Ulsterman** finished service in December 1967, becoming the accommodation ship **Cammell Laird** for Cammell Laird at Birkenhead, and later the Mediterranean Link Line's **Sounion**. Her career ended with an underwater explosion whilst moored at Beirut on 4 March 1973, awaiting the return of her American cruise passengers who were ashore sight seeing. Refloated on 17 April, she was sold for demolition.

Ironically the two elderly ferries had been displaced by new building for the Ardrossan route in the form of the car ferry **Lion** which arrived on station on 3 January 1968. The **Lion** was capable of carrying about 160 cars and 1200 one class passengers across to Belfast in just 4 hours, at a speed of 20 knots.

The Coast Lines Group commissioned two further diesel ferries in the 1930s. These were the **Leinster** and the **Munster**, which were destined for the Liverpool to Dublin overnight service and chartered to the British & Irish Steam Packet Company. Two-thirds of the cost of the new-buildings, some £380,000, was loaned by the Midland Bank and guaranteed by the Northern Ireland Ministry of Finance. The Northern Irish

Government required that ownership of the ships be retained by Coast Lines so both ships were registered initially at Liverpool, not at Dublin. Both ships, however, had Dublin on their stern before the outbreak of war. The **Leinster** was the first ship to be ready, and she carried out her maiden voyage on 4 November 1937 from Belfast to Liverpool on charter to the Belfast Steamship Company. The actual building cost of the ship was £293,690.

The new ships were slightly larger than the Burns & Laird Royals and were delivered wearing a garish buff hull with green boot topping and white upperworks, topped by a distinctive green white and black funnel. The white band was a new feature for the British & Irish ships. They again had a pronounced rake to the stem, the bridge front was stepped and the funnels were designed over large to give an appearance of power. However, neither the **Munster** or **Leinster** was equipped to carry cattle.

The passenger accommodation on the new Dublin boats was second to none. With saloon berths for 425 and berths also for 120 steerage class passengers, they clearly had an eye to an expanding passenger business. Much use was made of mahogany veneer in the saloon public rooms, and in the restaurant an overall grey theme was achieved with use of bleached oak and contrasting darker woods, complete with blue leather upholstery and a bright coloured floor covering. The smoke room walls were adorned with paintings of race horses, and the overall expression was one of luxury. The machinery was similar to that aboard the **Royal Ulsterman** and **Royal Scotsman**, except that the engines for the two Dublin boats had ten cylinders rather than eight. The bore and stroke was otherwise identical.

Catastrophe struck the **Munster** on 19 July 1938, when she collided with an American freighter off Anglesey in thick fog and a heavy swell. The damaged ferry was assisted back into Liverpool by the inbound **Ulster Prince**. Damage was largely confined to state rooms on the Promenade Deck, and injuries had fortunately been limited, with only one passenger requiring medical attention. The early months of the war saw the two ships laid up whilst a dispute with the crews over war risk pay was resolved. Sadly, the **Munster** was lost in 1940 when she struck a mine off the Mersey Bar, ironically whilst standing in on the Liverpool to Belfast service, an altogether premature end to a magnificent, and at that time neutral ship. The **Leinster** was taken out of lay-up at Barrow in April 1940 and her port of registration transferred from Dublin to Liverpool under the aegis of Coast Lines. She was then used as a hospital ship during the remainder of the hostilities, and was released from war service in 1945, to emerge in March 1946 resplendent in Belfast Steamship Company colours as the **Ulster Prince**, the new consort for the **Ulster Monarch** on the Liverpool to Belfast service. Transfer from Coast Lines ownership was effected for a sum of £300,000.

The **Ulster Prince** was hugely successful in her new role, and continued in service until September 1966, when she was renamed **Ulster Prince I**, releasing her name for the new car ferry which was soon to replace her. The final sailing of the **Ulster Prince I** for the company took place on 8 October, after which she was laid up at Birkenhead pending disposal. She was sold for demolition in Belgium, and sailed for Ghent on 8 April 1967, but was quickly sold on to Greek ship owners. Her subsequent life included work as a Mediterranean cruise ship **Adrias**, later **Odysseus**, a role in a film with Peter O'Toole and Sian Phillips in Venezuela, and finally as an accommodation ship at Kyle of Lochalsh. She was broken up at Faslane in 1979.

The temporarily-renamed **Ulster Prince 1** *(1937) laid up in the Morpeth Branch Dock, Birkenhead, during winter 1966/67.*

The first pair of second hand diesel ferries came into the British registry in 1937. These were the twins *Baltavier* and *Baltabor*, which dated from 1924, and which joined the fleet of the United Baltic Corporation, running between London and the Baltic. They had been built in Gothenburg as the *City of Panama* and the *City of San Fransisco* for the Pacific Mail Line of San Fransisco. Initially registered in Panama, to avoid the constraints of the American prohibition law, they served between the United States North Pacific ports and Panama. They were twin screw ships driven by two 12-cylinder Götaverken diesel engines which could maintain a service speed of 12 knots. They carried a mix of general cargo and passengers.

Sold to the Dollar Line in 1925, they continued on service, but were re-registered in San Fransisco during 1929. The pair were renamed in 1932, respectively *Santa Catalina* and *Santa Monica*, and again in 1936 becoming the *Chimu* and *Cumbal*. In September 1937 they were bought by the United Baltic Corporation for £32,000 each, entering service the following summer after extensive refits at Liverpool. This reduced their passenger capacity from 120 on the San Fransisco service to only 12, but all the original public rooms were kept available for the few passengers on the London service. It was not surprising that the pair quickly became popular with the travelling public, but the new career of the *Baltabor* was short-lived. Aground at Liepaja on passage from Riga to London in February 1939, she was not refloated until June, and was later declared a constructive total loss; all crew and passengers were landed safely during the incident.

The *Baltavia* became a naval stores carrier during the war, seeing service in South America and later between East Africa and Sri Lanka. She was reconditioned for civilian use in 1946 at Grimsby and remained on the Baltic service until 1957, when she was sold for further service out of Hong Kong. There she was eventually scrapped in 1964 under the name *Shun Siung*.

Towards the end of the 1930s, two identical sisters, the *Koningin Emma* and *Prinses Beatrix*, were completed by Koninklijke Maatschappij De Schelde for the Stoomvaart Mij Zeeland and their joint service with the London and North Eastern Railway to the Hook. They had twin De Schelde/Sulzer 10-cylinder diesels that produced 10,000 kW and gave the ships a service speed of 23 knots.

Also in 1939 the first of the British railway operators looked to diesel propulsion for a large ferry. However, the first diesel driven railway ferry was doubly innovative, as she was also the very first British, purpose-built, roll-on roll-off car ferry to be commissioned. This was the London, Midland & Scottish Railway ferry *Princess Victoria*, which was delivered by William Denny for the Stranraer to Larne crossing at a cost of £190,000. Her design reflected the ever increasing demand for the carriage of cars on the 'Short Sea Crossing'.

The *Princess Victoria* was powered by twin Sulzer diesels, each with 7-cylinders which had a bore of 48 mm and a stroke of 70 mm. The port engine was built by Sulzer at Winterthur and the starboard one locally by Denny. The engines could sustain a speed of over 19 knots, with a shaft speed of 252 revolutions per minute. The ship was of modest proportions by the standards of today, as she had a gross tonnage of only 2197 and a length of 94 m. She was launched from the yard of William Denny on 21 April 1939, and entered service on 7 July.

The builder's records include the following details:

Contract: For the Stranraer-Larne service. To carry 367 tons deadweight on 11 feet draft. Price £187,000. Delivery to be in 17 months.
Description : Plate keel, single bottom. Nine watertight bulkheads, to remain afloat with two compartments open to the sea. Fitted with a bow rudder, six 26 foot hand-propelled lifeboats, and two masts. Livestock carried on Lower Deck forward, ramp in the stern with cars accommodated in the 'tween decks.

The pedigree of the new ship was clearly one of a line of high class cross-channel ships, except that all the passenger accommodation was confined to the Promenade Deck and the Upper Deck, the Main Deck being largely given over to garage space. Passengers were divided, as usual, between first and third class, with a capacity respectively for 875 and 542 passengers. The garage could accommodate up to 65 cars, but the headroom on the car deck was only 3.7 m. There were two 6 m diameter turntables forward on which vehicles could be turned to face the stern ramp on loading or unloading. There were also cattle pens on the Lower Deck.

From the bows the *Princess Victoria* looked much like her steam driven consorts on the Stranraer to Larne route but aft she was dominated by the distinctive squared and flat topped stern complete with half deck swing gates which opened to provide vehicular access to the garage deck. This loading arrangement was a copy of that used on the Harwich- and Dover-based train ferries. Shore side ramps provided access to the car deck at all states of the tide, both at Stranraer and at Larne.

The new ship was equipped with every modern aid. She had a stern bridge and stern facing riding lights for the long passage up Loch Ryan, as well as a bow rudder to help with this manoeuvre. She had a crew of 44. Placed into service at the eve of war she only had two months on the route for which she was designed. This required a leisurely round trip per day, outward from Stranraer at 1900 hours and back the next morning at 1000 hours. The first car ferry was soon requisitioned as a minelayer, a duty for which her speed and stern door were well adapted, but was herself mined at the mouth of the Humber in May 1940, at the tender age of only 13 months. Only 85 of her war time crew of 121 survived.

Although British operators had been reluctant to adopt diesel propulsion for fast short sea vessels during the 1930s, other nations had been more adventurous. The reasons why the British ferry operators were dragging their feet included the confidence of the UK railway operators in steam, the relative low cost of coal in the UK, and the availability of steam engineers to man the vessels. There was also a feeling that diesel engines were synonymous with vibration and discomfort which was hard to dispel. By the end of the 1930s, diesel driven ferries had been championed in Canada, Argentina, Russia and Japan. Of all these nations, the Japanese were particularly advanced in ferry design and diesel manufacture, and Russia continued to spend a lot of effort on diesel engineering. Nevertheless, throughout the 1930s, the technology of Burmeiston & Wain and of Sulzer maintained them both as market leaders.

THE *ROYAL SCOTSMAN* AND *ROYAL ULSTERMAN* AT WAR

For much of the Second World War, the **Royal Scotsman** and the **Royal Ulsterman** were together, at times also in the company of the **Ulster Monarch**. In February 1942 the three ships sailed from Gibraltar, together with the Polish troop ship **Batory**, carrying Royal Air Force personnel bound for Takoradi and Lagos. The **Royal Scotsman** had to turn back to Gibraltar at this stage with generator trouble, and disembarked her troops at Bathurst; the **Ulster Monarch** later returned to pick them up. Lieutenant Commander W R K Clark takes up the story in an article first published in *Sea Breezes* in July 1946: The **Royal Ulsterman**, having disembarked troops at Takoradi and Lagos, sailed in company with the **Batory** to Takoradi. Here the **Royal Ulsterman**'s electric windlass failed to function with 75 fathoms of cable out on each anchor. Efforts to weigh by hand were thwarted at first by a pawl breaking on the hand gear. This was speedily repaired on shore and with the help of local troops both anchors were weighed the following day and the ship sailed for Freetown. Attempts to repair the windlass motor were not successful at Freetown, but in April the **Royal Ulsterman** proceeded to Simonstown, where the defect was remedied. At Durban the ship joined the force which had come from the UK to capture Diego Saurez and was assigned a special task, which consisted of proceeding astern of minesweepers into Courrier Bay, with the destroyers **HMS Lightning** and **HMS Loyal**, in close support to anchor 3 miles off the coast defences. While in this position detachments of the East Lancashire Regiment and No 5 Commando were landed and the batteries captured before they could open fire. The story continues with the **Royal Ulsterman**, **Royal Scotsman** and **Ulster Monarch** entering Gibraltar on the way south again, this time to North Africa, refuelling and sailing again during darkness in order "to disappoint curious eyes on the Spanish mainland". The three ships continued to the eastern flanks of Oran where the troops disembarked at Arzev. The **Royal Scotsman** and **Royal Ulsterman** then joined the Inshore (Moonlight) Squadron alongside two Dutch Zeeland Steamship Company diesel ferries which had become the British assault landing ships **Princess Beatrix** and **Queen Emma** (respectively the **Prinses Beatrix** and **Koningin Emma** in peace time – see Table 3). As such, the four ships helped maintain the Bona to Algiers ferry, which Clark describes as an exciting time for them and for their escorts: Manoeuvring by wireless telegraphy at night to avoid torpedoes was used on several occasions when the senior officer had decided that the squadron had been detected by enemy aircraft or submarines, that no useful purpose could be served by maintaining radio silence, and that manoeuvring by light signals was too dangerous. Aircraft which evaded the destroyers had a very warm reception from the ships in convoy and splashes of torpedoes dropped from aircraft and the tracks of both air and surface torpedoes became a commonplace sight. The **Royal Scotsman** and the **Royal Ulsterman** proceeded home in March 1943 for refit. The remainder of their war included Sicily, Salerno, Anzio and Normandy. The **Royal Ulsterman** was the Invasion Force Headquarters ship at the capitulation of the Channel Islands.

Table 3   Key pioneer diesel-driven ferries around the world

Ship	Owners	Year built	Grt	Speed (knots)	Comments
Ulster Monarch	Belfast Steamship Co Ltd	1929	3735	18	World's first diesel-driven passenger ferry
Ciudad de Asunciun	FANU (Argentina)	1930	2300	14	Two-stroke cycle diesel driven ferry
Kalundborg	Danish State Railways	1931	1400		Single-screw passenger ferry
Venus	Bergen Steamship Co	1931	5407	20	World's largest two-stroke cycle diesel ferry
Prince Baudouin	Belgian Government	1934	3050	25	World's fastest diesel ferry (Sulzer, two-stroke cycle)
Nishika Maru	Kansai (Japan)	1934	1800	16	Built and engined by Mitsubishi
Royal Scotsman	Burns & Laird	1936	3244	19	First British four-stroke cycle diesel ferry
Vega	Bergen Steamship Co	1938	7287		World's largest diesel ferry
Koningin Emma	Zeeland Steamship Co	1939	4136	23	High speed ferry - Sulzer engines
Princess Victoria	London, Midland & Scottish Railway	1939	2197	19	World's first diesel roll-on/roll-off ferry
Storebaelt	Danish State Railways	1939	2900	15	World's first diesel major train ferry
Kronprins Frederik	United Steamship Co	1940	3895	20	Last of the 1930s orders

Table 4   Diesel passenger vessels lost in World War II

Ship	Grt	Date lost	Place and cause of loss
Munster	3735	7 February 1940	Mined in Liverpool Bay
HMS Princess Victoria	2300	18 - 19 May 1940	Mined off the Humber estuary
Queen of the Channel	1400	28 May 1940	Attacked by aircraft at Dunkerque
Royal Sovereign	5407	9 December 1940	Mined in the Bristol Channel
Innisfallen	3050	21 December 1940	Mined off the entrance to Canada Dock, Liverpool
HMS Ulster Prince	1800	25 April 1941	Grounded at Nauplion, Greece, and attacked by aircraft
Royal Lady *	3244	6 May 1942	Attacked by aircraft at Gozo, near Malta

* Maltese owned

The **Ulster Queen** was declared beyond economic repair and scrapped after the war. In addition, 28 British diesel-driven coastal cargo ships and 3 coastal tankers were lost. The majority of these were owned by the Coast Lines Group and by F T Everard & Sons Ltd, both companies having invested heavily in motor ships during the 1930s.

CHAPTER 6

EXCURSION SHIPS AND SMALL FERRIES

The excursion and short estuarial ferry routes were traditionally the preserve of the paddle steamer. Broad in the beam, these relatively small ships were of shallow draft and very manoeuvrable in shallow waters. However, some operators on the Clyde had employed turbine engines since the very first turbine steamer, the **King Edward**, had emerged on the scene in 1901. In 1926, the innovative **King George V** was delivered for Clyde service, although this ship was very much a floating turbine test bed. Her original machinery proved to be over-ambitious, and demonstrated the unsuitability of water-tube boilers for estuarial duties, for which the boilers were forced up to full pressure for short periods between piers before again being damped back.

Another problem with the geared turbine steamers was the momentum of their massive gear trains. This made ships such as the **King George V** and **Marchioness of Graham** somewhat tardy at the piers, due to the time required to slow the gears before they could be put into reverse. It was for this reason that the Denny-built **Duchess of Montrose** was designed as a direct–drive turbine ship, based on the originally Edwardian engineering principle. She was followed two years later, in 1932, by sister **Duchess of Hamilton**. So confident were Denny of this second contract that they had already placed advance orders for steel and castings, only to find that they had been undercut in price by Harland & Wolff! Denny managed to persuade the Williamson-Buchanan partnership to take the third ship that had then to be built to use up the many parts they had already acquired. This was the rather palatial **Queen Mary**, completed by Denny in 1933, and built with the parts originally intended for the Caledonian Steam Packet Company's **Duchess of Hamilton**.

Bearing in mind that diesel ferries were already successfully in operation in the Western Isles (Chapter 4), it is surprising that the diesel engine did not get serious consideration over the turbine on the Clyde at this time. As compensation, the diesel-electric paddler **Talisman** came off the drawing boards in 1935 (Chapter 7), and a number of small ferries and excursion ships were built in the 1930s. Perhaps a main drawback of oil fuel was that the railway companies could buy coal in bulk at favourable cost, and that oil fuel was relatively expensive for them. Perhaps the stories of the vibrations aboard the **Lochfyne** and the **Ulster Monarch** were sufficient deterrent.

That being so, the pioneering work of the Coast Lines Group, and the development of the Southern Railway vehicle ferries for use at Portsmouth (Chapter 2), led to a flurry of orders for small diesel passenger ships, and passenger and vehicle ferries elsewhere. The first of these was the **Medina**, built to the order of the Southampton, Isle of Wight and South of England Royal Mail Steam Packet Company (Red Funnel Steamers) in 1931. Like so many of the ferries built for this company, the **Medina** came from the Southampton yard of J I Thornycroft & Company. She was a small vessel, only 43.6 m in length and with a gross tonnage of 347, but she had accommodation for 650 passengers and could take up to 10 cars on her open car deck aft. Surprisingly, her hull was slab-sided, with absolutely no tumblehome, making her vulnerable to damage whilst alongside in exposed waters. This largely prevented her from being used either as an excursion ship or as a tender. In addition she had a lively tendency to roll even in the light seas of Southampton Water; this reflected her relatively broad beam, which made her very stiff, although still a good sea boat.

The **Medina** was equipped with twin two stroke cycle 6-cylinder Gardner diesels, which drove twin shafts and gave her a modest speed of 10 knots. This inadequacy required her to be separately timetabled, as she could not maintain the faster schedules of the paddle steamers. Notwithstanding, the **Medina** gave her owners a good return on their investment, and was found to be a very economical unit. During the war she stayed on the ferry service without major mishap.

In 1950, representatives of Gardner's were called to ask what could be done to pep up the engines of the **Medina**. Even with slipping every four months to remove marine growth from the hull, the ship could not beat the 10 knot barrier. Re-engined and modernised in the winter of 1952/53 with twin engines made by Crossley Brothers of Manchester, she was at last able to maintain an enhanced service speed of 13 knots. At this stage, her gross tonnage was increased to 347. With her new engines she remained a profitable ship on the ferry service, until she was superseded by new roll-on roll-off tonnage in 1962, after which she had a new lease of life at Gibraltar, as the tender **Mons Abyla**.

Throughout the 1930s Gardner made two types of diesel engines, the larger powered two stroke direct reversing engine used originally in the **Medina**, and later in a number of small excursion ships, and also the smaller four stroke cycle 2-, 4-, 6- and 8-cylinder type for use in fishing boats and work boats. So robust were the latter that when E R Foden (ERF) was looking for a diesel engine for his new line of diesel lorries he found the only suitable engine to be the 75 kW Gardner four stroke marine engine. This is perhaps a unique example of a marine engine being adapted for road use, whereas nowadays the converse is commonplace, with road or industrial engines adapted for use in boats.

Between 1935 and 1938, a flurry of small diesel ferries and excursion boats were built for use on the Clyde and on Loch Awe for the Caledonian Steam Packet Company. All of these, however, were equipped with 4-cylinder Glasgow-built Gleniffer engines, with a stroke of 120 mm and a bore of 150 mm. The ships were the **Wee Cumbrae** for use on the Cumbrae ferry, the **Countess of Breadalbane**, initially used on Loch Awe but brought to the Clyde in 1952, later ending her days on Loch Lomond, as well as the two excursion boats **Ashton** and **Leven**. In addition the **Arran Mail**, which had a limited passenger capacity of 10, and was used on the Ardrossan to Brodick cargo (and cars) service, had two 6-cylinder Gleniffer engines with a slightly larger bore and stroke. Only the **Ashton** and **Leven** survive today, the former as the **Wyre Lady** based inland at Doncaster, and the latter, having recently returned from service in Jersey as the **Pride of the Bay**, now serves as the **Bristol Queen** at Weston-super-Mare. The **Arran Mail** was lost with her crew of five whilst on passage from Alderney to Newport in January 1962, then owned by Allen Shipping of Guernsey. Two other small motor passenger vessels from this era on the Clyde were the **Gay Queen** and **Maid of Bute**, which were built for service out of Rothesay.

Gleniffer diesels were also used to power the Lake Windermere boats **Teal** and **Swan**, built for the London, Midland & Scottish Railway in 1936 and 1938 respectively. These are the largest vessels on the lake and, with three decks, they were originally designed to carry 800 passengers in two classes. They are larger versions of the **Countess of Breadalbane**, and the twin diesels are coupled to twin shafts via 2 : 1 ratio reduction gearing. With a shaft speed of 480 revolutions per minute, the engines provide 240 kW, to give the vessels a speed of 11 knots.

Other little ships of similar vintage included the Hythe - Southampton ferries **Hotspur II** and **Hotspur III** which were built by the Rowhedge Ironworks Company in Essex in 1937 and 1938. However, both received new 4-cylinder Gardner engines in 1949. In the late 1930s, business was booming with the Imperial Airways Flying Boat Base established at Hythe, and not only was a 55 ton **Hotspur III** completed, but the **Carrick Lass** (Chapter 2) was bought from her Girvan owners and brought south. The latter was the only casualty of the war, when the ship that was transporting her to West Africa sunk.

A series of slightly larger diesel driven coastal excursion ships were built in the 1930s, each characterised by full length Promenade Decks and substantial Boat or Sun Decks. These included the **Royal Lady** built in 1934 for the Scarborough excursion trade, the **Brit** completed in 1935 for use at Great Yarmouth, the **Coronia** which was completed in 1935 for use at Scarborough, and the **St Silio** which was built in 1936 for use in North Wales.

The **Coronia** was built on the Humber, and was powered by twin four stroke cycle 6-cylinder engines built by the National Gas and Oil Engine Company. Originally sporting only one squat funnel, a second was added in 1937 to match the twin funnels of her competitor, the **Royal Lady**. Each ship carried a musical troupe, usually comprising piano, accordion and banjo. There was an amicable agreement that the ships should take turns at the favoured berth nearest the booking office at Scarborough. The competition was narrowed when the **Royal Lady** was replaced in time for the 1938 season with a bigger and faster vessel, the **New Royal Lady**. After serving as a patrol boat in the war, she was bought by the

The **Coronia** (1935) returning to Scarborough from an excursion in August 1967.

newly formed John Hall (Cruises) Limited, and spent the 1947 season on the Forth as the *Royal Lady*. A contemporary news report states:

"The main lounge will accommodate an orchestra, and the floor has been suitably surfaced for dancing, while from the band rostrum, music will be relayed throughout the ship. There is also restaurant accommodation for between 40 and 50 passengers, and in the after part of the ship is a special ladies lounge."

At the end of the season she was bought by the General Steam Navigation Company and given another new name. As the *Crested Eagle*, she was responsible for London Docks cruises until 1957, when she was sold to become the Maltese *Imperial Eagle*. Her twin Crossley diesels served her throughout a long career.

The *Brit* also served at Scarborough. Following a brief spell on the Thames after the war, she moved in 1951 to Scarborough to become the *Yorkshire Lady*. Although considerably rebuilt over the years, her Crossley diesels stayed with her until 1961, when she received a new pair of Gardner 6LX engines which gave her an increased speed of 12 knots. In 1968 she was renamed *Coronia*, the former ship of that name was sold to Crosons for use at Bournemouth the previous year. Under Crosons, the old *Coronia* was renamed *Bournemouth Queen*, but after only seven seasons she went to the Clyde as the *Queen of Scots* - see page 58.

The *St Silio* was similar in design to her east coast counterparts, although slightly bigger with a gross tonnage of 314. She made her first trip to North Wales on 27 May 1936, soon to inaugurate sailings from Amlwch as well as Menai Bridge and Llandudno, with occasional trips along the Manchester Ship Canal. She spent much of the war on the Mersey as an Admiralty inspection ship, and on return to civilian duties was given the more sensible name of *St Trillo*.

The **St Trillo** had two 6-cylinder, two stroke, single acting scavenge pump Crossley diesels. The engines developed 240 kW at 300 revolutions per minute, giving the ship a speed of 13 knots. The engines were of the direct-reversing type; the reversing mechanism was controlled by a single hand wheel. The only other control was the throttle. Each engine also drove its own compressor for start and manoeuvring air, and water pumps for cooling and general purposes. There were also two small auxiliary engines, one for electric power and a general service pump, the other for the hydraulic pump for deck machinery and an auxiliary air compressor.

*The **St Trillo** (1936) arrives at Menai Bridge in August 1967.*

The first captain of the *St Silio/St Trillo* was Captain J McNamee. He remained with his charge until September 1955, a period of almost twenty years; sadly terminal illness prevented him from completing the season. His ship continued for the Liverpool and North Wales Steamship Company until 1962, when the company was wound up. The *St Trillo* was able to continue under the auspices of P & A Campbell until 1969, but her faithful engines were beginning to show signs of wear, and the ship was by no means the reliable unit she once had been.

An innovative diesel driven excursion vessel was launched in 1935 by William Denny in partnership with the New Medway Steam Packet Company for service on the Thames. This was the *Queen of the Channel*, owned jointly by the two companies in the name of the newly formed London, Southend and Continental Shipping Company, and designed specifically for the long day trip, cross-channel excursions. The ship had developed from an approach by Denny to the Thames operator for a partnership with which to demonstrate the validity of a diesel-driven long-day excursion vessel.

The *Queen of the Channel* had a gross tonnage of 1162 and was slightly smaller than the famous 1932-built paddler *Royal Eagle*. The ship had twin 8-cylinder Sulzer diesels, which produced 920 kW at 320 revolutions per minute to drive the ship at 19 knots. There were two well proportioned yellow funnels, the forward one being a dummy. The ship was otherwise white with green boot topping and there were two thin green bands on the hull. Her accommodation was modelled partly on that of the **Royal Eagle**, but in layout the ship also resembled the Clyde steamer **Queen Mary**. The Promenade Deck of the **Queen of the Channel** was enclosed forward with large windows. The Boat Deck was continued aft almost to the stern of the ship to provide shelter to the Promenade Deck below. The Boat Deck also offered passenger access forward of the bridge.

The **Queen of the Channel** quickly established a reputation for comfort and service on Tilbury to Ostend, Calais or Boulogne day excursions, although comfort seems hard to visualise with a full complement of 1600 passengers. Within the first year, the New Medway Steam Packet Company managed to buy all the shares from Denny, and the London, Southend and Continental Shipping Company was dissolved. At the same time Denny was contracted to build a second motor vessel to be called the **Continental Queen**. This time a radical new design, which was to be repeated for all subsequent new builds for the Thames, incorporated a flared side like a paddle steamer's sponsons, whereby the uppermost three decks were carried out over the hull to give additional deck space. The superstructure was designed to provide maximum open deck and promenade area, with the Boat Deck continued over the forward lounge to provide a semicircular deck space before the bridge. The bridge, like that of the **Queen of the Channel**, was open to the elements, and was set well back, almost amidships. The ship had one large oval funnel, and there were two over-large ventilator cowls immediately aft of the funnel.

The new ship never sailed under her intended name, but emerged from the shipyard as the **Royal Sovereign**, because the New Medway Steam Packet Company had been bought by the General Steam Navigation Company whilst the ship was on the stocks. Delivered in time for the 1937 season, the **Royal Sovereign** displaced the **Queen of the Channel** from the Tilbury station enabling the latter to commence continental services from Great Yarmouth. The **Royal Sovereign** had a similar, but more powerful, propulsion system compared with the earlier ship, but was larger with a gross tonnage of 1527. Her design speed was 21 knots.

So successful were the two ships that a third variation on the theme was ordered from Denny. This was the **Royal Daffodil**, and she was launched on 24 January 1939. She was even larger, with 2060 tons gross, different in that her Boat Deck was continued almost to the stern, and with twin funnels. The new ship took up station at Tower Pier in April, running to Ostend, and returning her passengers by train connections at Tilbury in the late evening. Civilian duties were rudely interrupted towards the end of that first season. All three ships attended at Dunkerque; sadly the **Queen of the Channel** was bombed and broke her back before being abandoned at Dunkerque. The **Royal Sovereign** was later lost on contact with an acoustic mine in the Bristol Channel in December 1940.

*In August 1965, the **Royal Daffodil** (1939) is seen pulling away from Deal Pier.*

The **Royal Daffodil** survived alone, having rescued 9500 soldiers from Dunkerque, where she received bomb damage to her port engine, but later maintaining the Stranraer ferry alongside P&A Campbell's turbine excursion ship **Empress Queen**, before being transferred to Dover in 1944.

Released from duty in 1947, the **Royal Daffodil** received a covered bridge, permanent repairs to her port engine and the combined GSNC/New Medway Steam Packet Company emblem on the funnel, which was later changed to the GSNC house flag. She continued under the banner of Eagle Steamers on the Thames after the war, although only non-landing cruises to view the French coast were permitted until 1954. The last season, 1966, was described by a spokesman for the General Steam Navigation Company as grim, due to a combination of the strike of the National Union of Seamen and poor summer weather. The old ship was sold the following year for demolition. That she survived the rigours of war time, and sailed for so many years in her seasonal peace time role is testimony to both her design, and her machinery as well as the men who maintained and serviced her.

In 1939, the **Earl of Zetland** was completed for the North of Scotland, Orkney and Shetland Shipping Company by Hall, Russell at Aberdeen. Designed for the inter-island services in the Shetland Islands, based at Lerwick, she was equipped with just one engine, a 6-cylinder direct-reversing British Auxiliaries unit built at their Glasgow works, connected to a single shaft.

The war years were spent on the Pentland Firth crossing between Caithness and Orkney, and the new ship was seven years old before she finally took up her design route. Designed principally as a cargo and cattle carrier to service the needs of the many small islands in the Shetlands, she doubled as a passenger vessel as well. In this role, the **Earl of Zetland** had ample passenger accommodation for about 200, depending in later years on the season and whether she was operating on a Class 2a or a Class 3 passenger certificate. The fore part of the ship offered hold space and 'tween deck stalls for animals.

The **Earl of Zetland** (1939) at Lerwick in June 1974.

Eclipsed by new roll-on roll-off ferries operated by Shetland Islands Council, the **Earl of Zetland** completed her final trips to the islands in 1975. After service as an oil exploration survey ship, she assumed static duties at a variety of ports, ending up at North Shields where she lies to this day.

Three other important diesel ferries were commissioned just before the war. These were all equipped with the innovative German-designed Voith Schneider cycloidal propulsion units, a vertically mounted rotary blade propulsion system now widely adopted for use in estuarine waters. The first of these was the Red Funnel Isle of Wight ferry **Vecta** built by J I Thornycroft in 1938. Her twin 6-cylinder, four stroke English Electric engines could produce up to 925 kW to shafts at 325 revolutions per minute. Bevel gears were mounted directly above the vertical propulsion blades to reduce the speed of the blades to 135 revolutions per minute, giving a trials speed of 15.5 knots.

The **Vecta** (1938) arriving at Southampton's Royal Pier in July 1964. Designed with neither a rudder nor any means of reversing the main engines, the new **Vecta** was a highly manoeuvrable vessel.

The **Vecta** had a gross tonnage of 630, and could carry 855 passengers in two classes. First class passengers had a 60 seat dining saloon on the Main Deck, and a bar and forward facing observation lounge on the Promenade Deck. The second class lounge was aft and there was deck space forward, which was reserved for the carriage of about 14 cars. In 1939 she became a one-class ship and remained so until withdrawn from Southampton in 1965. At the start of the war, the spare parts for the Voith Schneider units were lost during a bombing raid, and this left the ship vulnerable to mechanical disorder. She set off, like so many other little ships, to Dunkerque, but had to abandon the trip and put back to Dover. Her war ended in January 1942, when she was laid up as unserviceable for lack of spares.

In 1946, the mothballs were shaken out and the stern of the ship was completely rebuilt. This time conventional twin propellers and a rudder were installed, driven by an electric couple from the original main engines. As a diesel-electric ship, she could now only attain just under 15 knots, but the electric couple gave a means of reversing and direct control from the bridge. The *Vecta* was not always a comfortable vessel, and suffered from excessive vibration. She was nevertheless used widely for excursions after the war, as well as the Cowes to Southampton ferry. She finished on 18 September 1965 on sale to P & A Campbell, and started in the Bristol Channel the following week, still with her shiny red and black funnel. The following year she re-emerged in Campbell livery under the name *Westward Ho*, but was reduced to a static role in Manchester in 1972.

Another Isle of Wight ferry, the double ended vehicle ferry *Lymington*, was built at a cost of £30,000 for the Southern Railway in 1938. She was of 295 tons gross, and could carry 20 cars and up to 400 passengers. She was also given twin Voith Schneider units, and, like the *Vecta*, she too suffered considerable mechanical difficulties in her early days. A product of William Denny, the *Lymington* had two cycloidal units, one fore and one aft, which were connected to twin 6-cylinder four stroke type 6S30 engines built by W H Allen at Bedford. The *Lymington* started service in the Lymington River on 1 May, almost a year before the *Vecta* which was then still having trouble completing the installation of her Voith Schneider units. However, of the first twelve months' service of the *Lymington*, eight were spent laid up awaiting parts or under repair. The main problem was driftwood damage to the blades. The original six-bladed equipment was replaced in the 1950s with new four-bladed units, but her engines saw her through to the end.

The *Lymington* remained on station until displaced by larger tonnage in 1974. She was then sold for the same price as she had originally cost to build, to Western Ferries (Argyll) Limited for use on the Clyde as the *Sound of Sanda*, a second career which she successfully maintained for nearly twenty years.

The third pre-war unit to be fitted with Voith Schneider blades was the Dundee to Newport vehicle ferry *Abercraig*. Manoeuvrability was a prime consideration on this service which was traditionally the preserve of small paddle steamers. The *Abercraig* was launched in October 1939 from the Paisley yard of Fleming and Ferguson. She had two 8-cylinder engines each cylinder with a bore of 248 mm and a stroke of 267 mm. A little larger than the *Lymington*, she had a gross tonnage of 455 and had cost £55,000 to build. She could accommodate 1200 passengers and 45 cars.

Known locally as the "jinx ship", the *Abercraig* struggled as the Tay ferry throughout the war from one breakdown to another. Dependent on a local engineer, James Forrester, who seemed to have mastered the mechanics of the novel propulsion system, she was finally laid up when the new road bridge opened in 1966. Unlike the *Lymington*, she did not realise her building costs and was sold, along with her post-war sister the *Scotscraig* (Chapter 8), for demolition for a paltry £15,000. Many of the modern inshore and estuarine ferries are equipped with Voith Schneider units, including all the present day Isle of Wight vehicle ferries.

With the *Vecta* safely laid up for much of the war, and both the *Lymington* and the *Abercraig* retained on their design routes, all three had survived the hostilities that had broken out as these ships first entered service. A great many other short sea vessels were not to return to their civilian duties, and with them a great many of their crews, officers and men, had lost their lives in the service of the nation.

On a July day in 1964, the **Lymington** *(1939) approaches the town from which she took her name.*

CHAPTER 7

PADDLE 'STEAMERS'

The diesel-electric coupling had been proved in the screw driven ferries **Lochfyne** and **Lochnevis** (Chapter 4). It was yet to be applied to side paddle vessels. The first estuarine ferries to use diesel, coupled with electric motors and chain-drive to independent paddle wheels, were the Forth vehicle ferries **Queen Margaret** and **Robert the Bruce**. They were built by Denny for Denny, the London & North Eastern Railway having given the lease for the North to South Queensferry crossing to the shipbuilder conditional on his constructing the new ships.

The two new ships were both launched on 25 January 1934. The **Robert the Bruce** was the first all electrically welded ship to be built in Scotland, whereas her sister retained traditional riveted construction by way of comparison. The pair were otherwise identical. Although they had a gross tonnage of only 228, they could carry 500 passengers and 28 cars, loaded via ramps over the side from the adjacent slipway. They were double-ended vessels and the sponsons continued the length of the ships to provide enhanced deck space.

The **Mary Queen of Scots** *is seen on builder's trials in the Firth of Clyde.*
(University of Glasgow)

The main engines aboard each ship were a pair of Davey-Paxman 8-cylinder four stroke single acting engines with a bore of 165 mm and a stroke of 255 mm. The electric chain drive couple to the paddle wheels (which were capable of independent operation) allowed the diesels running at 750 revolutions per minute, to drive the paddle wheels at an efficient 45 revolutions per minute. A third almost identical ship was built by Denny in 1949. Post-war shortages prevented this one from retaining the electric couple, and the new ship, the **Mary Queen of Scots**, was equipped with diesel-hydraulic drive, again connected to the paddle wheels by chain. She had Crossley Brothers' 8-cylinder, two stroke single acting engines with a cylinder bore of 180 mm and a stroke of 230 mm. The hydraulic link included a hydraulic clutch to control speed and direction. Interestingly, this arrangement gave her a speed (if required) of 11 knots against her earlier diesel electric sisters' 8 knots. A fourth and slightly larger vessel was built in 1956, the **Sir William Wallace**, and she too had this same combination of machinery. The opening of the Forth Road Bridge ended the ferry service in 1964. The three older ships were scrapped, but the **Sir William Wallace** saw further service in the Netherlands.

The most famous diesel-electric driven paddler was the **Talisman**, built to the order of the London & North Eastern Railway by A & J Inglis of Glasgow for £48,900 in 1935. Inglis had always been very involved with the North British Railway and latterly with the London & North Eastern Railway. However, Inglis, along with Fairfields, were the two chosen tenderers out of an initial list of thirteen, and Inglis reportedly only won the contract after they submitted a letter claiming a mistake in their tender to bring their price just below that of their competitor. Apparently Fairfields retaliated with a revised bid of £48,000, but by then the machinery layout suggested by Inglis had gained favour with the LNER Committee. Bidding in those days, of course, was an overt affair which lent itself to such unscrupulous behaviour.

The **Talisman** was launched on 14 April by Evelyn Whitelaw, daughter of the Chairman. The **Talisman** was affectionately known as the 'clockwork mouse'; her machinery was never satisfactory and it failed her completely in the middle of the 1939 season. The traditional appearance of the Clyde paddle steamer, this one with a gross tonnage of 544, was marred only by the concentrated racket from her engines and the noisy discharge of the exhaust gases from her single funnel. The funnel was originally adorned with a navy type cowl to disperse the noise of the engines. Described by George Stromier as "a quaint gadget, for all the world like a giant tiddlywink", it had little effect on subduing the engine noise and was removed in 1936.

The *Talisman* was designed to carry 822 passengers in winter and 1590 in summer with a crew of 21. She was equipped with four sets of 8-cylinder four stroke cycle airless injection engines with a bore of 255 mm and a stroke of 312 mm, and coupled via a pair of generators to two electric motors, with the armatures connected directly onto the shaft between the paddle wheels. The paddles could not be operated independently, a safeguard against failure of one side or other which would render the ship unmanageable, but possibly a reflection also of conservatism by the Scottish masters. The generators were designed to run at 600 revolutions per minute, and supplied direct current to the motors, which in turn drove the paddle shaft at 50 revolutions per minute. The machinery, including the four diesel units, was built by English Electric at Stafford. A design problem meant that she lay in the water when the way was off her, requiring much heaving on the lines to adjust her position at pier heads.

The **Talisman** *in her first year of service.*

(Alistair Deayton collection)

The 1935-built **Talisman** *minus her 'tiddlywink' funnel cowl as seen in 1939.*

(Alistair Deayton collection)

On trials the *Talisman* recorded over 17 knots, but on service 14 knots was achievable with only two of the diesels running. At 17 knots she achieved a crash stop overrun in just 2$\frac{1}{2}$ lengths. Accepted from her builders, she undertook an inaugural cruise under Captain McVicar on 21 June, and speeches claimed great things of the ship, including manoeuvrability equivalent to an extra half knot between the piers. Interestingly, the main instrument board was placed adjacent to the main motor room, for passengers to observe the revolutions, electrical current and power that was being produced. The economics of the machinery are illustrated by fuel consumption compared to the conventional paddle steamer of the same name which the diesel-electric ship replaced. On a comparable journey and speed, the *Talisman* of 1935 burned only one eighth of the equivalent calorific value of fuel than the *Talisman* of 1896, a vessel of the same length but of slightly less displacement than the new ship.

There were two reasons behind the strange design of the *Talisman*. One was that the shallow water off the LNER pier at Craigendoran was such that turbine steamers (already in service with the Caledonian Steam Packet Company at Gourock) would be of too deep a draft to access the pier. The *Talisman* had a design draft of only 2.0 metres. The second was probably a desire by the LNER to impress its potential customers with the appeal of exciting new diesel technology. The preferred design, therefore, had to be for a shallow draft paddle vessel. Her layout was not unlike any other paddle steamer of the day save that her first class accommodation was situated forward of the paddle boxes. She had a full length Promenade Deck, a cruiser stern and a straight stem with little flare forward. The lack of flare was highlighted by plated bulwarks which were initially painted black, but which were replaced by railings in post-war years.

Initially praised as a most efficient vessel (in her first year she sailed 41,000 kilometres at an average speed of 15 knots at a cost of 24 old pence per kilometre), she soon began to develop mechanical problems. But even during this initial honeymoon she was never a popular ship with passengers who were suspicious of her machinery and wary of its noise. By 1936 her original innovative curved steel paddle floats had had to be replaced with conventional flat wooden ones. But, during her 1937 overhaul, all of her diesel engines were found to have cracks in and around the water cooling jackets. Modifications recommended by English Electric were rejected by the owners, and make-do welding saw her back on duty in time for the winter service.

Only two years later, in 1939, a crack developed in the water jacket of the No 1 starboard engine, such that circulation had to be discontinued. Instead of shutting down the engine and running on the remaining three for the rest of the season, the affected cylinder was isolated and the unbalanced engine was kept in service! Seven weeks later the shaft fractured (not a great surprise), and another water jacket cracked on one of the port side engines. Her passenger certificate was withdrawn, and she was laid up at Bowling on 28 July, at the height of the season.

Repair work was completed by English Electric in May 1940. She was then converted by Inglis for use by the Admiralty, losing her own name which was already in use by a destroyer. As she left the quayside on 28 September to undertake sea trials, the LNER Marine Superintendent Captain Perry reportedly uttered the caustic farewell "Take her away and don't bring her back!". During the war the paddle vessel saw service as **HMS Aristocrat**, initially as a Bofors gun anti-aircraft platform in the Thames, and later in the raid on Dieppe, as a protection ship in preparations for the North Africa landings, and finally as HQ ship for the construction of Mulberry harbour sections. She returned to UK waters in June 1945, but was not released from duty until early 1946.

In his book *Craigendoran Steamers*, (see reference section), Alan Brown described the post-war plans for the new paddle steamer **Waverley** as follows :

"It is interesting to note that, 12 years after the construction of the **Talisman** the question of burning oil in the cylinders of an internal combustion engine and driving the paddles via an electric motor was not even deemed worthy of consideration. The appointment of Captain Perry in September 1937 had coincided exactly with **Talisman**'s first major breakdown, and the trials and tribulations experienced with the diesel-electric ship had left very deep scars. Despite an unblemished war time record Captain Perry's attitude to **Talisman** remained one of complete mistrust, and steam alone was specified for the **Waverley** in 1946."

Despite the Marine Superintendent, the **Talisman** was back on the Clyde in time for summer 1946. Now with a new bridge housing and her bulwarks removed, her first commercial voyage saw her limp back into Craigendoran with engine failure. Although her machinery had held up well throughout the harsh years of the war, it was again her downfall in peacetime as she could now only attain 15 knots. She soon earned the reputation of "slow boat to Rothesay" and, by June 1953, the poor condition of her diesel units and general need of a thorough overhaul was such that she had to be withdrawn and laid up, most likely to be disposed of. Her champion and saviour was Captain Colin MacKay who had been impressed by the ship and suggested that she be re-engined as a replacement for the ailing **Marchioness of Lorne**.

During the winter of 1953/1954, the **Talisman** received four 8-cylinder diesels built by British Polar Engines at Glasgow, with the same electric couple to the paddle wheels. The cylinders on the new engines had a bore of 100 mm and a stroke of 300 mm. This new arrangement reduced her service speed still further to only 12 knots, although she attained 15 knots on trial at 46 revolutions per minute shaft speed. In the end she was retained because of her useful large passenger complement and she was able to provide valuable service on the seasonal Millport service. In 1966, her final year in service, the old lady could only manage reduced power owing to generator failure and shortage of parts; she made her final public sailing on 17 November 1966, and was sold to for demolition at Dalmuir the following year.

One further large diesel electric unit was built after the war. This was the **Farringford**, which was built to the order of Southern Railway in 1947 by William Denny & Brothers of Dumbarton, for service between Lymington and Yarmouth on the Isle of Wight. Although the **Lymington** had been built for this service before the war and equipped with German-manufactured Voith-Schneider propellers, such equipment was not available in the immediate post-war era (Chapter 6). The paddle motor vessel **Farringford** was launched on 21 March 1947. She had a drive-through vehicle deck with loading ramps fore and aft and a high amidships superstructure. The sponsons were continued for the full length of the ship, and the paddle boxes were concealed so that her appearance bore little resemblance to a conventional paddle steamer.

The paddles were independently driven by separate electric motors. There were four rudders, two at each end of the ship. Twin generators supplied 225 kW direct current at 350 volts, and were in turn driven by two 6-cylinder single acting, four stroke cycle, 6SKM Crossley diesel engines, the electrical equipment being supplied by the English Electric Company at Stafford. The ship had a gross tonnage of 489, and could maintain a service speed of just over 10 knots, with the engines developing 315 kW at 650 revolutions per minute. She was at that time the largest ship to operate out of the Lymington River, and there was some public concern that she might be too big. She nevertheless quickly developed a reputation for punctuality, and within two months of commencing operation, broke all records by carrying over 4500 passengers in one day.

The passenger accommodation comprised two separate lounges, perched high and overhanging the car deck, one to port and the other to starboard, with room between for high-sided vehicles to pass. On top was the wheelhouse and two pole masts. The *Farringford* was licensed to carry 812 passengers, cattle and goods, or 320 passengers and 32 cars. She was one of the first ferries in UK waters not to offer passengers any access to outside deck space, a feature that has been on the increase in recent years. In 1959, another Voith-Schneider propelled vessel, the *Freshwater,* joined the fleet, but, throughout all, the paddler *Farringford* maintained reliability second to none. Her manoeuvrability was as good as that of the Voith Schneider ferries, save that she could not move sideways off the quay as they could.

The carriage of cattle on the *Farringford* and her running mates was often the cause of entertainment for the passengers. In an article in *Sea Breezes*, Eric Payne reported:

"As an instance, there was the cow that jumped from the quay and swam quickly out to sea followed by rescuers in five dinghies. After about 100 yards the animal was secured by a rope and towed back to shore, but not before it had kicked out causing one dinghy to be overturned throwing the occupants into the sea."

The service was not entirely without mishap; the weather in this part of the Solent can, on occasion, be quite severe, and the approach to the Lymington River is rather narrow. Caught by a gust of wind in the twisting approach to the river, the *Farringford* was more than once stranded for a few hours awaiting the tide to lift her off a sand bank. In October 1967, she left Yarmouth one night at 1800 hours into a growing gale, only to turn back and spend her one and only night at Yarmouth.

Both the paddler and the elderly *Lymington* were withdrawn from the route in 1973. The *Farringford* was then converted to side loading, and her end loading ramps were welded shut and cut down to the top of the bulwarks. Transferred to the Humber, she was able to maintain the Hull to New Holland ferry, initially alongside the one remaining steam paddle ferry, *Lincoln Castle*, but later alone. On completion of the Humber Road Bridge, the *Farringford* was withdrawn, with nine years of Humber service to her credit, and laid up. The last Humber crossing took place on 26 June 1981. The *Farringford* was eventually demolished in 1984 as lying at Hull.

A diesel-electric paddle vessel of sorts was built for the Sandquay Point to Old Rock chain ferry on the River Dart, and given the exotic name of *Dartmouth Higher Ferry*. The system was also used by the Admiralty for a series of seven tugs known as the Director-class. They were built between 1956 and 1957, specifically to handle large overhanging ships such as aircraft carriers. They were each equipped with 12-cylinder Davey-Paxman oil engines driving generators and motors, with chain drive to independently operating paddle wheels. It is noteworthy that the Admiralty favoured the diesel-electric couple, rather than the diesel-hydraulic couple which had then been used successfully on the Forth vehicle ferries. The new tugs replaced a variety of elderly steam paddle tugs, and were deployed both at home and overseas, the *Dextrous* doubling as a harbour tug at Gibraltar and attending the visiting cruise liners that occasionally called at the port at that time.

*The **Farringford** (1947) in the Lymington River during July 1964.*

CHAPTER 8

POST-WAR REBUILDING

There was intense competition for shipyard resources and materials in the latter part of the 1940s, even though post-war inflation had significantly increased the cost of shipbuilding from the depressed prices of the 1930s. For example, the Dundee Harbour Trustees were able to order a repeat of the **Abercraig**, once parts were again available from Germany for the Voith Schneider cycloidal units. The new ferry was built at the yard of Caledon Shipbuilding & Engineering of Dundee, and was eventually delivered in 1951 at a cost of £171 000, considerably more than the pre-war cost of £55 000 for the **Abercraig**. Named **Scotscraig**, the only significant difference between the ships was her main engines, which were twin 6-cylinder units with a bore of 254 mm and a stroke of 312 mm.

The railways embarked on a major replacement programme for war-time losses. Nationalised in 1948, and subject to the conservative influence of government, the newbuildings were largely turbine steamers based on pre-war design. The **Falaise** and **Normannia**, for example, were variations on the Southern Railway flagship, **Invicta**, which had been completed in 1940. There were, however, three large diesel passenger units built at this time: the new **Princess Victoria** for the Stranraer station, and the passenger mailships **Cambria** and **Hibernia** for the Holyhead to Dun Laoghaire route.

Other operators had already eschewed the turbine for the diesel engine. The Coast Lines Group, for example, desperately needed new tonnage, and they too set about a rebuilding programme for the Cork and Dublin services. The General Steam Navigation Company needed to replace its excursion ships that had been lost in the war and David MacBrayne also needed new tonnage. All of these companies ordered diesel powered ships.

Only one diesel powered coastal vessel was built in the UK during the war with an eye to later being adapted for passenger use, although a number of military ships built in the war were later to be adapted for civilian passenger use (Chapter 10). The one was the Burns & Laird Lines' **Lairds Loch**, completed in 1944 by the Ardrossan Dockyard, and equipped with a pair of British Auxiliaries 8-cylinder engines. She was completed as a cargo carrier, as war-time restrictions did not permit the building of a passenger ship. The **Lairds Loch** (known as the "Derry Dipper") ran trials on 30 August 1944, and immediately took up service on the Derry to Glasgow route, taking some twelve hours for the overnight crossing at a speed of 13 knots.

The **Lairds Loch** returned to her builders in the winter of 1947/48 to be converted for passenger use. Now remeasured at 1709 tons gross, she emerged with single and double cabin accommodation for 44 saloon and 8 steerage class passengers, the latter usually reserved for women. There was a small dining saloon and a small bar/lounge forward for saloon passengers, and similar facilities in the 'tween deck for steerage passengers. There was still room for the same volume of cargo including stalls for up to 350 cattle during the winter. In the summer the cattle stalls were removed from the 'tween decks to make room for up to 700 steerage class passengers, and rows of seats were installed on the Main Deck; a further 300 saloon class passengers were also carried. No cargo would be

Glasgow's Broomielaw Quay is the setting for this view of the **Lairds Loch** (1944) in 1964.

carried with this large passenger complement, but conditions aboard could hardly be considered comfortable on a twelve hour passage in such a small ship across exposed waters. In September 1966, the Derry passenger service was closed, and the **Lairds Loch** transferred to the Glasgow to Dublin passenger service until the **Irish Coast** (Chapter 11) returned from relief duties elsewhere. Thereafter, the **Lairds Loch** carried only cargo and cattle until she was sold to Israeli owners in 1969. She was beached the following year and abandoned in the Gulf of Aqaba as a result of a commando raid.

David MacBrayne had been awarded a mail contract in December 1938 which required two new ships. The first had been the **Lochiel** (Chapter 4), but the order for the second was delayed by the war, and plans for this new ship, for the outer isles service based at Mallaig, were finally displayed to the Provost of Stornoway and his councillors in February 1945. William Denny was contracted to build the new ship. Some 18 months later, following protracted delays caused by shortages of materials, the new **Loch Seaforth** finally entered the water on 19 May 1947. Her maiden voyage was further delayed during fitting out, and took place on 6 December.

The link between Denny and Sulzer continued with the installation of twin 6-cylinder type 6TS36 Sulzer diesels, together generating 900 kW, and giving the **Loch Seaforth** a service speed of 16 knots. The ship was a distinctive and imposing vessel for her size, with the accommodation occupying the after two thirds of the vessel. Capable of carrying 500 passengers in two classes, she also had space for 36 cattle within a total of 680 cubic metres of cargo space. The first class lounge was particularly attractive, with large windows looking forward from the Boat Deck.

Mallaig is a very photogenic location. Here we see the **Loch Seaforth** *(1947) arriving from the outer isles during August 1970.*

The **Loch Seaforth** was off service briefly in 1965 following grounding at Kyle of Lochalsh. She was later transferred from her design route to the Oban to Outer Isles service. Three further minor groundings occurred to the ship. Then, under Captain Donald Gunn, on her normal Thursday morning return run from Lochboisdale and Castlebay to Oban via Coll and Tiree on 22 March 1973, the **Loch Seaforth** ran aground on the Cleit Rock, Gunna Sound, between Coll and Tiree, sending out a Mayday call just after 0515 hours. The 28 crew and 11 passengers took safely to the ship's boats. The ship was refloated with tug assistance later in the day, and towed to Scarinish, where she settled on the bottom in 6 m of water. She was later salvaged and towed to Troon where the wreck was declared a constructive total loss and sold for demolition. Coincidentally, the David MacBrayne cargo vessel **Loch Carron** also went aground four days after the **Loch Seaforth**, this time at Lochboisdale. The **Loch Carron**, however, was salvaged and quickly put back into service.

The first of the larger post-war ferries to be delivered was the new **Princess Victoria**. This ship was almost identical to the pre-war vessel of the same name that was lost in the war (Chapter 5). Built for the London, Midland & Scottish Railway, the new **Princess Victoria** became part of the Scottish Region of the nationalised system of railways from 1948 onwards. The only discernible external difference between the two ships was the position of the radio direction finder mast on the bridge house, that in the new ship being aft of the position on the original vessel. Otherwise, the dimensions of the ship were identical, she was again Denny built, and she was equipped with the same twin 7-cylinder Sulzer engines as before. The new **Princess Victoria** had a greater amount of space given over to passenger accommodation, and was consequently measured with an increased gross tonnage of 2694, against the 2197 gross tons of the original vessel.

The new stern-loading car ferry **Princess Victoria** adopted the seasonal morning sailing from Larne and evening departure from Stranraer, in support of the traditional passenger turbine mailship **Princess Margaret**. The car ferry also maintained the year round service for transport of milk road tankers, bringing full loads to Scotland and returning the empties in addition to relieving on the mail service in the off-season. In 1952, it was proposed that the **Princess Margaret** be transferred to Belfast for a new service to Stranraer with passengers and cargo only, and that the car ferry develop a year round service for passengers and vehicles between Larne and Stranraer. However, opposition from various public services prevented this development ever taking place.

A trials view of the second **Princess Victoria**, *built in 1946.*

(University of Glasgow)

Whilst instrumental in developing the roll-on roll-off traffic between Northern Ireland and Scotland, the ship was to have a very short life. On Saturday 31 January 1953, she left Stranraer at 0745 hours, and headed down Loch Ryan into a south-easterly gale. No sooner had she left the shelter of the Loch than she ran into difficulties, as following waves stove in her small half deck, horizontally hinged doors. The first SOS was transmitted at 0930 hours, and the impending disaster became national news for the remainder of the day, as people sat listening to radio news bulletins about the ship's predicament. On her beam ends, the ship foundered sometime during the afternoon before help could arrive. She had managed to run towards the shelter of the Irish coast, but was unable to turn around into the gale, and she sank 8 km off the Copeland Islands. There were only forty three survivors, all relatively young men, and of the 139 lives that were lost, many were women and children. Included in the list of dead were the MP for North Down, Sir Walter Smiles, the Northern Ireland Minister of Finance, Major Maynard Sinclair Sinclair and the master, Captain James Ferguson.

At the subsequent Inquiry it was revealed that the scuppers on the car deck were inadequate to remove the volumes of water cascading through the breached stern doors. The tragedy prevented the railways building further passenger and vehicle ferries of this design, other than train ferries, until the turbine steamer **Caledonian Princess** was completed (also for the Stranraer route) in April 1961. The turbine driven car ferry **Lord Warden** was commissioned at Dover prior to the disaster. However, the **Princess Victoria** disaster was only the first of many car ferry tragedies. Although she showed the need for scuppers of sufficient capacity to discharge water from the car deck, it was to be many years before the realisation that watertight bow and stern doors, vehicle deck subdivision and cambered vehicle decks would ensure the security of this type of vessel.

The next conventional diesel driven railway ferries were the **Hibernia** and **Cambria**, built by Harland & Wolff of Belfast for the British Transport Commission, newly formed with the nationalisation of the railways. An article by Cyril Yeates, first published in *Sea Breezes* in January 1967, included the following introduction to the sisters:

"One fine day in April 1949 there sailed into the Inner Harbour at Holyhead the motorship **Hibernia** to introduce to the astounded inhabitants of that port the 'new look' in mail ships. Large, bulky and tall but, none the less, handsome she was completely devoid of the slender grace and beauty of the old **Hibernia** which she had come to replace. . . licensed to carry 2000 passengers in two classes, and owing to its size it has been possible to provide ample saloon and promenading space for day crossings and adequate sleeping accommodation for night travellers ranging from double berth de-luxe staterooms in the first class to six berth cabins and open berths in the second class. The **Hibernia** made her maiden crossing (to Dun Laoghaire) on 14 April followed by the **Cambria** in May, and in service they both proved to be excellent sea boats but with a tendency to roll. This disturbing "idiosyncrasy" (in truth, a design failure) was soon curbed by the installation of Denny Brown stabilizers during the annual refit in 1951."

The 'new look' was in fact far from new, and followed closely an enlarged version of the design set by the builders for the Coast Lines Seaway standard class of diesel cross-channel ferry (Chapters 3 and 5). It was, however, quite unique for the railways. The **Cambria** and **Hibernia** were designed with a service speed of

*A classic view of the **Hibernla** (1948) off the Holyhead breakwater on a sunny day in September 1974.*

*The **Cambria** (1948) arrives at Holyhead in August 1967.*

21 knots (4 knots less than the turbine steamers they replaced), but were then the largest and fastest British cross-channel motorships. They had twin Harland & Wolff/Burmeister & Wain single acting 8-cylinder engines which provided 8000 kW. The original gross tonnage was 4972, but was remeasured in 1965 at 5284, following a major refurbishment and upgrading of the passenger accommodation. The original order for replacement tonnage on this route had been placed in 1939 with Fairfield Engineering for two turbine driven vessels, an order later cancelled with the onset of war.

The most significant departure from the Coast Lines' standard ship design was that all the passenger accommodation was amidships. This was a departure from the convention of placing steerage class passengers aft, a practice still retained in the contemporary **Munster** and **Leinster** which were completed in 1948 (see below). The other difference from these British & Irish vessels was that the new Holyhead sisters had no provision for the carriage of cattle. At both the 1965 refurbishment and during other major refits, the first class accommodation was reduced at the expense of second class, so that the ships eventually became almost one class. Cabins on C Deck were stripped out to make way for new second class lounges amidships and aft, and a second class smoke room replaced first class cabins on D Deck. In addition the B Deck smokerooms for first and second class became a 146 seat tea room, and a new second class lounge was constructed aft of the main lounge. Finally, side screens were fitted to provide additional enclosed deck space on A Deck. As built, the fittings were very traditional, with widespread use of hardwood finishes; on the bunk boards at the head of every berth was the traditional velvet pad and hook on which the sleeping passenger could hang their watch for the night.

The **Cambria** very nearly came to grief in her first year of service. Entering Dun Laoghaire harbour in fog, she struck the pier and, story has it, heeled over to 25º before righting herself. Not one plate was left in one piece in the galley! With the hole plugged by concrete and later inspected by a diver, the **Cambria** limped across the Irish Sea to Cammell Laird for repairs, the voyage reported to have taken 11 hours to complete.

The two-ship mail boat service (2045 hours from Dun Laoghaire and 0315 hours from Holyhead), which allowed passengers to sleep on board until 0600 hours, was taken over by a vehicle ferry as from October 1975. The **Cambria** had completed her last voyage on 7 September, and the **Hibernia** continued until 3 October the following year. A well-advertised farewell cruise round Dublin Bay with tickets at £15 a head came to nothing, and the ship finally left Dun Laoghaire with a single exchange of siren with the new steam turbine driven car ferry **Dover**. It was estimated that the **Hibernia** had carried 12 million passengers during her 27 years on the Irish Sea. The **Hibernia** was sold to Greek shipowners, who never used the ship, and resold her for demolition in 1981, and the **Cambria** was mainly used in the seasonal pilgrim trade to Jeddah until she sank at her moorings off Suez in 1980.

The **Leinster** and **Munster** (respectively 4115 and 4088 gross tons) were ordered in December 1945 from Harland & Wolf for the British & Irish Coast Lines service between Liverpool and Dublin. Unlike the pre-war ships of the same name (the former **Leinster** had now become the **Ulster Prince** on the Belfast route, and the **Munster** had been lost off the Mersey early in the war – Chapter 5), the new ships had stalls for up to 480 cattle, as well as considerable refrigerated space. The cattle were carried from Dublin to the lairage at Birkenhead Woodside before the ships crossed the river to Princes Dock.

The **Munster** was launched on 25 March 1947 and the **Leinster** followed on 20 May. The pair was delivered ready to commence on the Liverpool to Dublin route on 5 April 1948, the **Munster** having spent the previous month on the Cork to Fishguard route. Access to Princes Dock remained tidal until March 1950, so a third ship was required to cover for vessels that could not complete loading in time to move into the river to load passengers at Princes Landing Stage. This was usually the **Longford**, formerly the **Lady Connaught** and originally the **Heroic** dating from 1906.

The **Munster** and **Leinster** carried a distinctive and striking livery: buff superstructure with a green hull and a yellow line, with orange boot topping. The funnel colours were green and black top separated by a white band. First class passengers were accommodated amidships. There were single and twin berth cabins for 225 although single cabins were later modified to increase the number of first class berths to 265 passengers. They had access to a smoke room and lounge on the Boat Deck and a drawing room on A Deck. The dining saloon, the Purser's office and the reception hall were on B Deck. Third class passenger accommodation remained aft (in contrast to the contemporary Holyhead sisters **Hibernia** and **Cambria**). There were two and four berth cabins for 107 third class passengers, but with a passenger certificates of 700 first class and 800 third class, space in the public rooms for unberthed passengers (especially in third class) was at a premium, particularly during the Christmas period.

Sailing were 2200 hours from Liverpool and 2000 hours from Dublin. The early Irish departure allowed for the lay over at Birkenhead the next morning to offload cattle, before the scheduled 0700 hours passenger disembarkation time at Princes Dock. Arrival in Dublin was normally at 0730 hours. In later years a limited number of passengers' cars were carried, craned on and off at either terminal, and which had to be on the quay seven hours prior to sailing! There were no Sunday sailings. Cargo vessels also ran on the service from 1961 as back up for car carrying during the summer season.

The 1948-built **Munster** *is seen in the once-familiar surrounding of Princes Dock, Liverpool, in July 1964 wearing the distinctive green and yellow livery used by the company.*

The area has now been redeveloped and is the site of hotels and retail outlets, the fate of many former quayside areas.

The ships enjoyed relatively uneventful lives apart from minor groundings and collisions, Mersey ferries being a particular hazard. Outwardly, they only changed in appearance following sale by Coast Lines of B&I to the Irish Government for £3.6 million in January 1965; they adopted the colours of the City of Cork Steam Packet Company save for a defaced funnel with the new B+I logo applied in orange during the next winter overhaul. Displaced by new roll-on roll-off tonnage, the **Munster** ended her service on the Irish Sea as she had begun with a brief stint relieving on the Cork route in October 1967, and the **Leinster** followed her into lay up at Birkenhead just over one year later.

*The **Leinster** (1948) goes astern through Princes Half Tide Dock during her morning arrival at Liverpool from Dublin.*

The **Munster** was bought by Epirotiki Lines of Greece, and, as the **Theseus** and later the **Orpheus**, had a whole new career as a cruise ship before her. With cabin accommodation for only 370 in 155 cabins, and given full air conditioning, extensions to the superstructure fore and aft, plus a swimming pool in the aft well deck and a new bow, she was all but a new ship. Visiting West Africa and Alaska, she later became very well-known for her charter work to Swan Hellenic in the Greek islands, and was only broken up in 2000. The **Leinster** was sold for use as a Greek ferry under the name **Aphrodite**, and was altered to carry 100 cars and only 550 passengers. Laid up in 1983, she was sold for demolition in 1987.

A departure from building with Harland & Wolff for the Coast Lines group was the Denny-built ferry **Innisfallen** for the Cork to Fishguard route. She replaced a predecessor of the same name lost in the war (Chapter 5). Similar in many ways to the **Leinster** and **Munster**, the **Innisfallen** was smaller with a gross tonnage of 3705. She was launched on 12 December 1947 and delivered in June 1948, and after calling at both Liverpool and Dublin, she carried out her maiden voyage from Cork on 28 June.

Denny equipped the **Innisfallen** with a pair of Sulzer two-stroke single acting trunk piston engines which gave her a service speed of 17 knots. Passenger accommodation included the normal lounge and smoke room and a large dining saloon which could seat up to ninety. Each first class cabin contained a chair and a small desk on which there was always a postcard of the ship, and beside the sink was a jug of drinking water. As with the Dublin ships, space for unberthed passengers on premium sailings was scarce, and the ship could often feel crowded. She had a number of novel features including electric radiant heating in the cabins,

*The **Innisfallen** (1948) alongside at Fishguard harbour in August 1963.*

and was built complete with Denny-Brown stabilizers. Her hull was subdivided into eight water tight compartments. She had three separate holds, including 210 cubic metres of refrigerated space in Number 3 hold. Cattle were carried in the 'tween decks. Displaced from the route in October 1968, she became the Greek inter-island ferry **Poseidonia**, but remained little altered during the remainder of her life. She was sold for demolition in 1985.

There were two other Denny built diesel ships built in the immediate post-war period. These were the Thames excursion ships **Royal Sovereign** and **Queen of the Channel**. They were essentially a development from the pre-war ships **Royal Sovereign** and **Royal Daffodil**, and like them continued the combination of Denny built with Sulzer diesels. The **Royal Sovereign** was delivered in July 1948 season and was followed in May 1949 by her slightly smaller running mate, the **Queen of the Channel**. Both ships were capable of maintaining 19 knots, with the **Royal Sovereign** capable of 20 knots when time and tide demanded. They could accommodate 1500 and 1900 day passengers respectively. It was quickly found by their owners, the General Steam Navigation Company, that there was now a surplus of tonnage on the Thames. The venerable paddle steamer **Golden Eagle** was laid up at the end of the 1949 season, and the newer **Royal Eagle**, completed only in 1932, was withdrawn in mid-season during the following year. The motor ships were able to rule the Thames for the next fifteen years, along with their pre-war sister the **Royal Daffodil** (Chapter 6).

*The **Queen of the Channel** (1949) leaves Southend Pier at the end of August 1966.*

Having provided great pleasure to several generations of Londoners, it was apparent by the mid 1960s that pleasure sailing to Southend, Margate or Calais was no longer as popular as it had been in the past. In 1966, in an attempt to revitalise income, the **Royal Sovereign** was redeployed from down-the-Thames sailings from Tower Pier to operate for the season out of Great Yarmouth. For the first time the new roster took the **Royal Sovereign** to France. The other two ships remained on the Thames, with the **Royal Daffodil** maintaining the French services. Sadly the National Union of Seamen's strike prevented services starting until June, and, to stem further losses, the excursion services were closed at the end of the season, and the ships were advertised for sale. So came to an end 142 years of pleasure sailings on the Thames. The General Steam Navigation Company had bought its first pair of steamers, the **Royal Sovereign** and **City of London**, in 1824, the year the company was formed, for the London to Margate and Ramsgate service.

It appears that closure of the services to France was welcomed by the British Embassy in Paris. During 1965 the Foreign Office brought pressure to bear on GSNC to restrict sales of alcohol on the outward voyages to France as there was mounting concern over the rowdy behaviour of many of the passengers whilst they were ashore at Calais and other destinations!

The **Queen of the Channel** survived in Greek waters as the **Oia** until withdrawn and demolished in 1984. The **Royal Sovereign** was quickly sold to the Stanhope Steamship Company for £100 000. She was cut down for use as a freighter with berths for 12 lorry drivers, given the name **Autocarrier**, and deployed on the Dover to Zeebrugge route then being developed by Townsend Brothers. She had an inauspicious start; entering service on 30 August 1967, her engines failed on the first return trip, and she limped back to Dover some nine hours out of Zeebrugge. Worse followed on 28 October, when she went aground outside the mole at Zeebrugge, with her engines running at full speed. Bent propellers and crooked shafts, flooded steering compartment and buckled plating put her out of action for quite a while. Nevertheless, she soon became a useful unit in the Townsend fleet, generally running to capacity with freight units. Resold in 1973, she became the **Ischia**, and was deployed on the Naples to Ischia ferry which she serves to this day.

*An impressive view of the distinctive **Autocarrier** (1948), formerly the excursion ship **Royal Sovereign**, off Dover in 1968.*

TROOP TRANSPORT *EMPIRE WANSBECK*

Completed by Danziger Werft AG of Danzig in 1943 as the **Linz** (the keel was laid in 1939), she became a war prize at the end of the war and was given the name **Empire Wansbeck**. She was put to work on the Harwich to Hook trooping run, along with the elderly railway steamer **Vienna** and the former Canadian National Railway steamer **Empire Parkeston**. The **Linz** had been quipped with one 6-cylinder double acting MAN diesel, which gave her a service speed of 15 knots and the capability of 16 knots. Her gross tonnage was little over 2562. As the **Empire Wansbeck** she could accommodate up to 1050 troops and other passengers on the seven or eight hour nightly crossing.

She was managed for the Ministry of Transport by Ellerman's Wilson Line. There was considerable rivalry between the motor ship and her steam consorts, with the **Empire Parkeston** described at the time as an expensive and inefficient white elephant. The assertion was that the larger steamer, albeit in former civilian life a luxury Canadian coastal cruising steamer, had a smaller payload (995 troops and other passengers) with less efficient engines and greater down time due to maintenance. The supporting evidence, however, remains slightly less obvious. Could it be that, as the **Empire Parkeston** was managed and manned by the General Steam Navigation Company, the rivalry was company based and not a true reflection of the ability of each vessel? All three ships nevertheless performed a valuable service for the troops then stationed in Germany.

The **Vienna** ended her working career on 11 February 1952, when a boiler explosion occurred alongside at Harwich, killing two of her crew. In due course, at the end of the trooping service, the **Empire Parkeston** was sold for scrap in 1962, but the **Empire Wansbeck** was sold for further service in Greek waters under the name **Esperos**. As such she was finally towed out of Piraeus on 14 March 1980, en route to a Spanish ship-breaking yard.

CHAPTER 9

CARGO WITH A FEW PASSENGERS

Until World War Two a number of 'coastal passenger liners' maintained services in competition with the railways. They offered relatively cheap fares and a leisurely, but enjoyable, means of travel. The key routes were between London, the north-east of England, Leith, Grangemouth, Dundee and Aberdeen, and between London, south-east England, Ireland and Liverpool. There was also a passenger route between Belfast and north-east England via Stornoway. Competition from the roads as well as the railways, plus the onset of the Depression in the 1930s, put a great deal of pressure on the services. However, three of the routes evolved with new 12 passenger diesel cargo liners, which had engines aft and the passenger and crew accommodation in a central island.

Routes which received the new 12-passenger ships were the Liverpool to London service, the Liverpool to Belfast and north-east England service and the London to Aberdeen route. The Liverpool service was maintained by the elderly steamship **Southern Coast** until she was displaced in 1936. She had been built for the Hough Line in 1911 before that company merged with the Powell and the Bacon lines to become Coast Lines. The **Southern Coast** could carry 80 passengers. She was joined on the route by the diesel cargo liners **British Coast** and **Atlantic Coast**, built in 1933 and 1934, and forerunners of a group of Coast Lines vessels which were to be built over the next fifteen years.

The **British Coast** and **Atlantic Coast** were of 890 tons gross and were built by Henry Robb of Leith. Twin-screw vessels, they each had a pair of 5-cylinder Polar direct-reversing diesel engines, built by British Auxiliaries Limited at Glasgow, which provided a service speed of 12 knots. The cylinder bore was 348 mm and the stroke 575 mm. The two ships were transferred to the Scotland, north-east England service in 1935 when the next pair were delivered: the **Pacific Coast** and **Ocean Coast**. These vessels regularly called at Falmouth, Plymouth and Southampton as required, offering their passengers a voyage within a roster that involved a seven day trip.

A company postcard from the 1930s advertising summer cruises between London and Liverpool by the **British Coast** (1933).

(Coast Lines Limited)

Another postcard produced by the company, this time showing the **Pacific Coast** of 1947.

(Coast Lines Limited)

The **Pacific Coast** and **Ocean Coast** were products of the Ardrossan Dockyard Company and Henry Robb respectively. They were equipped to carry 10 passengers. These were twin screw vessels with the same pairs of 5-cylinder direct-reversing Polar diesels, but their service speed was slightly slower than the older ships, at only 11 knots. They were slightly larger and were registered as having a capacity of 1173 gross tons.

The **British Coast** and **Atlantic Coast** took up service between Liverpool and Middlesbrough. This had formerly been operated by the Antrim Iron Ore Company whose ships had previously been absorbed within the Coast Lines empire. Leaving Liverpool on a Wednesday afternoon, they were scheduled to arrive at Middlesbrough the following Tuesday, having called at Stornoway and Leith. Return ports could include Newcastle, Dundee, Aberdeen and Belfast. The service was not continued after the war, and the two vessels were redeployed on the Kircaldy linoleum run, no longer offering passenger space, until they were withdrawn. The **Atlantic Coast** went to South African owners in 1962, and was resold for further service under the Italian flag in 1969, then 35 years old. The **British Coast** went to Canadian owners in 1963.

The **Pacific Coast** was lost right at the start of the war whilst carrying cased petrol to France. The cargo caught fire whilst she was lying at Brest, and, although salvaged and towed back to Falmouth, the ship was later broken up. A new vessel of the same name was completed by the Ardrossan Dockyard in 1947. The new **Pacific Coast** could accommodate 12 passengers. She was equipped with two 6-cylinder British Polar engines.

The third route to receive diesel cargo passenger liners was London to Aberdeen. The Aberdeen Steam Navigation Company maintained their elderly steamer **Aberdonian** on this service. Dating from 1909 and with accommodation for 80 first class and 200 second class passengers, she was replaced by the **Aberdonian Coast** which was built in 1946. A second vessel, the **Caledonian Coast**, was also ordered. Problems were immediately encountered, with the passenger schedule conflicting with the unpredictable nature of cargo working, and the service was quickly abandoned with the new ship transferring to the Coast Lines' London to Liverpool service under the name **Hibernian Coast**. Her new sister joined her at Liverpool in 1948, straight from Hall Russell at Aberdeen, the builder of the two ships. The two vessels could carry 11 passengers in what was described at the time as 'comfortable accommodation'. They were equipped with two sets of 4-cylinder direct-reversing British Polar engines built in Glasgow.

In January 1966, the **Caledonian Coast** (1948) enters the River Mersey from Liverpool's Trafalgar Lock.

In the 1960s, the **Ocean Coast** and the **Pacific Coast** departed West Trafalgar Dock, Liverpool, for Falmouth, Southampton, and London's East India Dock and came back via Cork and occasionally Belfast. The slightly faster **Caledonian Coast** and **Hibernian Coast** called at Plymouth on the way south and Dublin on the return. The return fare was about £50 providing five to six nights at sea. One of the best known characters from this era was Captain G Maerns, who used to regale his passengers with anecdotes in the dining saloon.

The **Ocean Coast** was sold in 1964 to Greek owners. The **Pacific Coast** continued in service slightly longer under the Red Ensign, with the seasonal task of carrying passengers' cars between Liverpool and Dublin between 1962 and 1966, in support of the **Leinster** and **Munster**, prior to the delivery of new roll-on roll-off vessels (see Chapter 8). In this role she could carry about 50 cars, and her passenger accommodation was always full. Her running mate for much of this work was the cargo only **Mersey Coast**, a 10 knot diesel engined ship dating from 1938, and typical of many of the early diesel cargo units in the Coast Lines fleet, but which had been occupied for much of her career on the London to the Channel Islands cargo service. Charter work occupied part of the off-season, during which the **Pacific Coast** undertook a number of voyages out of Hull for the United Baltic Corporation, and to the Mediterranean for the Brocklebank Line. Right at the end of her Coast Lines career, a problem occurred with carbon monoxide build up from a faulty domestic boiler; two passengers were killed in the incident on the first night out of Liverpool bound for London. The **Pacific Coast** was sold shortly afterwards for further service under Kuwaiti ownership.

The **Caledonian Coast** closed the passenger service in 1967, and was temporarily employed on the Brocklebank Line service to the Mediterranean as the **Makalla**, before being sold to foreign owners. The **Hibernian Coast** followed her overseas, after protracted lay up in Nelson Dock at Liverpool. The two ships were succeeded on the coastal service by the engines aft cargo only vessels **Lancashire Coast** and **Cheshire Coast**.

One other vessel of essentially similar design was built for the North of Scotland, Orkney and Shetland Shipping Company. This was the **St Clement**, built in 1946 by Hall, Russell of Aberdeen, broadly on the same lines as the twelve-passenger Coast Lines' ships of the same era. However, she only had one engine, a 6-cylinder direct-reversing British Polar engine, connected to a single shaft. Cabin accommodation centred on a small, dark, wood-panelled dining saloon which was the social hub of the vessel. The **St Clement** maintained the Leith to Thurso and Wick service until it was discontinued in 1955, and then she maintained the Leith to Orkney service and the Aberdeen to Kirkwall (Orkney) and Lerwick (Shetland) route, finishing in early December 1976. Strangely, accommodation could only be arranged via the cargo handing department at each port, and many enquiries to the passenger department at Aberdeen led to disappointment. Mini-cruises were available from Leith to both the main islands of Shetland and Orkney with or without hotel accommodation on one or other island between voyages.

A second diesel cargo vessel, also with accommodation for twelve passengers, was completed in March 1955 at Hall, Russell's Aberdeen yard. This was the **St Rognvald**, distinguished in having not only her engine aft, but also the wheelhouse and accommodation. She had originally been designed and ordered in 1952, with a likely passenger complement of about 200, for the Aberdeen to Wick and Orkney service. However, changing conditions dictated a need for only a few passengers, working partly out of Leith, and the **St Rognvald** was principally used on the cargo route between Aberdeen and Kirkwall, but was also deployed from time to time on the Leith to Shetland and Orkney services. Again the wooden panelled dining saloon was situated beneath the bridge and was adjacent to the eight single and two double berth cabins.

The service speed of the **St Rognvald** was 13 knots, providing an 11 hour passage between Aberdeen and Kirkwall. Nicknamed "The Flier", her engine was built for a passenger ship and was capable of sustaining a speed 16 knots, albeit with greatly increased fuel consumption, but providing useful capacity when chasing the tide at Leith on the way south from Aberdeen. Supplied by Denny of Dumbarton, the engine was an 8-cylinder direct-reversing Sulzer unit with an output of 1500 kW. Harbour manoeuvring on departure was invariably accompanied by clouds of smoke, which only settled down once the ship was clear of the harbour and full ahead had been rung down. The final departure of the vessel from Kirkwall took place in May 1978 under the command of Captain Andrew Georgeson, after which the ship was sold for further use under the name **Winston**.

*The **St Rognvald** (1955) arrives at Kirkwall in August 1968.*

Burns and Laird Lines had the cargo and cattle carrier **Lairdsglen** built for the Glasgow to Dublin service in 1954 as the successor to the **Lairdshill**. Completed at the Ardrossan Dockyard, she was equipped with twin Clark-Sulzer diesels. At the time it was stated that she would be converted for dual cargo and passenger working, depending on future requirements on the route. In the event, the conversion for passenger carrying never materialised, although she was converted for sole use as a cattle carrier in 1969, before being sold out of the fleet in 1974.

Two of David Macbrayne's cargo ships used on the Glasgow to the Outer Hebrides mail service were given accommodation for four passengers. These were the **Lochdunvegan**, built in Gothenburg in 1946 as the **Örnen** and equipped with a 5-cylinder Atlas Polar diesel connected to a variable pitch propeller, and the **Loch Carron**, built at Ardrossan in 1951, which had a 6-cylinder British Polar engine. They could manage 10 and 11 knots respectively. The older ship was bought second hand in 1950, the younger, of similar proportions, was built to the order of David MacBrayne. The service was reduced to a single ship in 1973, and closed in 1976.

The railways took little interest in diesel propulsion for cargo vessels until after the war. One of the more interesting vessels was the **Winchester**, which cost £215, 000 to build, and was a cargo ship with accommodation for 11 passengers. She had a peculiarly high forward profile and was, by way of contrast, correspondingly low towards the stern. The **Winchester** was powered by twin Sulzer direct-reversing engines, continuing the association between Denny and Sulzer inaugurated with the pre-war Thames excursion ships (Chapter 6). However, the resounding compressed air start on the diesels was extremely loud and very distinctive. Although she

*Built for the Southern Railway, the **Winchester** (1947) sets out from Southampton at the start of a voyage to the Channel Islands in June 1968.*

was an excellent and easily-handled vessel, the compressed air tended to run out after about twenty consecutive forward and reverse engine manoeuvres, a consideration which meant that an approach to Weymouth harbour in anything other than a light breeze had to be carefully planned! The **Winchester** remained on the Channel Isles services until 1971 when she was sold for conversion for use as a cruise ship in the Mediterranean. She was broken up only in 1996.

Only two other post-war conventional general cargo ships regularly carried passengers for the railways. These were the **Elk** and **Moose**, built also for the Channel Islands services, and completed by Brooke Marine Limited of Lowestoft in 1959. The ships each cost £408,000, nearly double the price of the **Winchester**, built twelve years earlier. The pair had twin 6-cylinder engines which gave them a service speed of 14 knots. Both ships were designed with a view to carrying twelve passengers on the Southampton service, but their switch to the Weymouth station early in their careers meant that this capability was never properly utilised. The main passenger role for the **Elk** comprised winter reliefs on the Jersey and Guernsey to St Malo service normally operated by the small turbine steamer **Brittany**, and latterly by the **St Patrick**, until the passenger service was closed in 1964. The **Elk** (or very occasionally the **Moose**) was advertised to carry ten male passengers who shared the dining saloon with the crew as a communal lounge for the duration of the relatively short voyage. Women, apparently, could not be accommodated. The **Elk** and **Moose** were sold overseas in 1972; the **Elk** foundered only four years later.

Associated Humber Lines, operating out of Goole and the Humber, offered twelve berths on its services to Bremen and Hamburg, and to Copenhagen. These services were operated by the **Whitby Abbey** and **Fountains Abbey**, which both came from Hall, Russell of Aberdeen in 1954, and the **Kirkham Abbey** and **Byland Abbey** which were built by Austin & Pickersgill of Sunderland in 1956 and 1957. All four ships offered high standard accommodation in six twin berth cabins. The former pair were equipped with twin 6-cylinder Kincaid-Polar engines, and the latter with twin 9-cylinder Ruston and Hornsby engines, single reduction gearing and hydraulic coupling. The ships had a speed of just under 13 knots. They were modest vessels by today's standards with gross tonnage of 1197 for the first two and 1372 for the younger pair.

Following the sale of the **Waverley** into preservation in the 1970s, Caledonian MacBrayne sought to continue the tradition of Clyde cruising by converting the **Glen Sannox** for this purpose. Although not suited to the role, she had a small but dedicated following and her crew certainly made their passengers very welcome. On 25 July 1978, she was photographed as she left Gourock on her way to Dunoon with a "streaker" in the distance. (Bernard McCall)

On the following day, the **Queen of Scots** is seen at Largs. This small excursion vessel, completed in 1935, served very different parts of the UK. Originally named **Coronia**, she served Scarborough until sold to Crosons for use at Bournemouth in 1967, being renamed **Bournemouth Queen**. She moved to Scotland in the mid-1970s and was renamed **Queen of Scots**.

(Bernard McCall)

The attempt by Western Ferries to develop a foothold amongst the Caledonian and MacBrayne routes proved to be unsuccessful except on the Clyde. The company's **Sound of Islay** (1969) was photographed approaching Port Askaig on Islay at the end of a voyage from Kennacraig on 30 July 1978. It is evident that her passenger accommodation did not match that available on more traditional ferries. Despite the shortcomings, the ferry built up a loyal following. *(Bernard McCall)*

To celebrate her twentieth year of service, the **Iona** (1970) made a special cruise around Arran and paid a most unusual visit to Ardrishaig on Loch Fyne. The date was 7 April 1990, and the ship is seen at Brodick Pier on the island of Arran.

(Bernard McCall)

Great rivers often have great landmarks. This is certainly the case on the Mersey where the "Three Graces" of the Royal Liver Building, Cunard Building and Port of Liverpool Building dominate the Liverpool skyline. These form a fitting backdrop for the **Royal Iris** (1950) on 24 July 1990 when over a quarter of a million people lined the river banks to see the **Queen Elizabeth 2** anchored in mid-river. *(Bernard McCall)*

What a contrast! This view of another vessel long associated with the Mersey, the **Ulster Monarch** of 1929, is taken from a company postcard. The caption reads "M.V. **Ulster Monarch**, 3,000 tons, has a luxurious lounge, comfortable smoke room, and spacious dining saloon. De-luxe, single and two berth cabins are available for over 400 first class passengers." *(Author's collection)*

The "Southern Corridor" across the Irish Sea has been the setting for intense competition in recent times. The traditional railway route from Fishguard has found it more difficult to maintain its market position as an increasing number of passengers have used motor vehicles. It has also suffered from having to use ferries built for other routes. A typical example is the **Earl Harold** of 1971, built for the Stranraer - Larne crossing as **Ailsa Princess**. She was photographed leaving Fishguard in October 1988.

(Bernard McCall)

Road access to Pembroke Dock is a little better than that to Fishguard and this has been exploited by Fishguard's rivals. On a sunny 12 May 1990, the **Munster** of 1969, then working in the colours of B&I Line, passes Angle Bay on her way through Milford Haven from Pembroke Dock.

(Bernard McCall)

Possibly the most-photographed of the North Sea Ferries fleet because of her work in the South Atlantic during the Falklands campaign, the **Norland** *(1974) is seen approaching the lock in Hull on an evening departure in 1978. Her passengers always watched with interest as she was manoeuvred skilfully into the lock, often in very inclement weather.*

(Bernard McCall)

The modal switch from rail to road transport and the use of the Channel Tunnel for the rail transport that remains has seen the demise of the rail ferry in southern England. Serving as a reminder of a previous generation, the **Cambridge Ferry** *(1963) is seen moored to buoys off Harwich on the hazy morning light of 4 June 1982.* *(Bernard McCall)*

The late 1970s and 1980s saw a huge surge in demand for travel on the shortest English Channel crossing between Dover and Calais. New ships were introduced by the main operators, Townsend Thoresen and Sealink. The **Spirit of Free Enterprise** (1979) was one of a class of three vessels introduced on the route by Townsend Thoresen. She is seen approaching Calais on 1 August 1986. *(Bernard McCall)*

On the same day, the **St Anselm** of 1980 leaves Calais at the start of a voyage to Dover. She was also one of three similar vessels but there are many evident design differences between her and her rival in the photograph above. The livery represented an attempt to move away from the "railway image" but the white paint was rarely in the condition seen on Scandinavian and Mediterranean ferries. *(Bernard McCall)*

The **Whitby Abbey** and **Fountains Abbey** maintained the Associated Humber Lines' services between Hull and Germany. The **Fountains Abbey** was abandoned at sea on 12 February 1962, when fire broke out in Number 1 hold during a strong gale on passage from Bremen and Hamburg to Hull. Attempts to fight the fire failed, and, with sparks shooting from the forward ventilators, Captain F W Wooler gave the order to abandon the vessel. Twenty of the crew of twenty two were saved by one of two trawlers which came to the rescue. There were no passengers aboard at the time. Later towed into port, the burnt out hulk was sold for demolition as unrepairable. Captain Wooler had been in charge of the ship since she was first commissioned. The **Whitby Abbey** continued until 1968, when she was sold for conversion to the 400-passenger Philippine registered inter-island ferry **West Leyte**.

The Copenhagen ships, **Kirkham Abbey** and **Byland Abbey**, were based at Goole and were operated for the British Transport Commission and, as such, did not carry the red band with black AHL on their funnels. They were also distinctive in having grey hulls rather than the company standard black. Transferred to the Ellerman's Wilson Line in 1965, they became the **Ariosto** and **Angelo** and were transferred to London, until sold in 1970, eventually to be broken up in 1983 and 1980 respectively.

A fine view of the **Kirkham Abbey** *(1956) in her final guise as* **Maldive Importer**.

(Bernard McCall collection)

There were also several short sea diesel vessels in service under the flags of Ellerman's Wilson Line and Currie Line Limited. All of these were built by Henry Robb at Leith and were equipped to carry 12 passengers in single and double berth cabins. They were the sisters **Cavallo** and **Trentino** dating from 1951 and the **Aaro** which was built in 1960, all for the Ellerman's Wilson Line services between Hull and Scandinavian ports, and the **Zealand** which was commissioned in 1955 for the Currie Line service between Leith, Germany and Denmark, and later used on the London to Lisbon service.

The General Steam Navigation Company offered limited accommodation for a few passengers on selected routes to the Continent during the summer months. MacAndrews' services to Iberia and the Mediterranean also offered up to twelve berths for discerning travellers, and their associate company, the United Baltic Corporation, offered some passenger berths on its cargo routes to Scandinavian ports out of London.

The only other 12-passenger diesel cargo ferries operated under the British flag in the 1950s and 1960s were the train ferries which served between Harwich and Zeebrugge. The limited passenger accommodation was provided principally for accompanied road vehicles, a role which became more important as time went on. The first pair were the **Suffolk Ferry** and **Norfolk Ferry**, which were built as replacements for the elderly **Train Ferry No 2** and **Train Ferry No 3**, which had been lost in the war. The **Train Ferry No 1** survived, and was refurbished after the war to emerge as the **Essex Ferry**. The original service had operated from Richborough in Kent, but was transferred to Harwich in 1924 under the Great Eastern Train Ferry Company. The new **Suffolk Ferry** was delivered to the London & North Eastern Railway by John Brown & Company of Clyebank in September 1947, and was followed by the **Norfolk Ferry**, which undertook her maiden voyage on 17 July 1951, the latter built to the order of the British Railways Board.

A contemporary account which first appeared in the *Railway Magazine*, September 1951, introduced the **Norfolk Ferry** as follows:

"Following experience with the **Suffolk Ferry**, the new ship has a similar form below the waterline, though the forward superstructure has been modified. A feature of the design already applied on the **Suffolk Ferry** is that the Upper Deck, which extends for almost the whole length of the vessel, serves as a cover for the Train Deck, on which the rail vehicles are secured. Four lines of track are provided for the accommodation of freight wagons on a deck constructed to be capable of supporting the heaviest type of modern locomotive. These lines converge into two embarkation tracks at the after end of the vessel only, the forward end being of the normal ship's form. As in the **Suffolk Ferry** the side tracks are 98.5 m long and the centre tracks 103.5 m long, giving a total of 343 m. The number of wagons which can be accommodated varies according to the size of wagon used, but the average number conveyed is between 32 and 38. Officers and crew are accommodated on the Upper Deck; in addition six, two berth cabins are set apart for the use of passengers. The **Norfolk Ferry** is a twin screw vessel designed to maintain a service speed of 13 knots when fully loaded."

During the early 1950s, the train ferry service to Zeebrugge went from strength to strength. The veteran **Essex Ferry** which had been completed along with her two sisters in 1917 by Armstrong Whitworth of Newcastle, was replaced in 1956 by a new **Essex Ferry**, and a fourth member of the fleet, the **Cambridge Ferry** followed in 1963. The ships were essentially similar, although slightly different in appearance.

The engines for the **Norfolk Ferry** and **Suffolk Ferry** were built by John Brown and comprised two stroke single acting engines with 6-cylinders each with a bore of 481 mm and stroke of 712 mm. The **Essex Ferry** differed in that she had twin Sulzer TS48 engines, built under licence by John Brown, which gave her a service speed of 13 knots at 300 revolutions per minute. The **Cambridge Ferry** was different again: a product of Hawthorn Leslie on the Tyne, she had Mirrlees National 7-cylinder diesels connecting to twin controlled pitch propellers via single reduction gears. She was also the first ferry to be fitted with flume stabilizers. In appearance she had a tapered funnel and a more modern appearance than the three older ships. The older vessels were withdrawn in the early 1980s. The **Cambridge Ferry** was used on a variety of routes after the Harwich service was closed in January 1987, and was sold in 1992 for further service as a vehicle ferry in the Mediterranean.

With a rail tank and road tank visible on her open stern section, the **Norfolk Ferry** (1951) leaves the train ferry berth at Old Harwich on 31 August 1974.

The 1956-built **Essex Ferry** sets out from the same berth on 8 April 1974.

EARLY DIESEL CARGO FERRIES

Once again the Coast Lines Group led the way with introducing the diesel engine, this time bringing the diesel to short-sea services operated on a cargo only basis. The first pair of ships was the **Fife Coast** and **Carrick Coast**. Small ships of only 367 tons gross, they had twin screws and 4-cylinder British Kromhout engines, later replaced in the **Fife Coast** with 4-cylinder Atlas Polar diesels. Although the **Carrick Coast** had electrically operated winches, those on the **Fife Coast** were petrol driven. The two ships entered service in 1933, and were the immediate predecessor to the **British Coast** series. By the War, Coast Lines had repeated this same midships accommodation, engines aft design for much of their cargo fleet, and more were built in later years either for Coast Lines or for its many subsidiaries.

Burns & Laird Lines and British & Irish stuck with the more traditional central island and midships engines for their cargo and livestock carriers. The first three motor cargo ships were the **Lairdswood**, **Lairdscrest** and **Lairdsbank** all built in 1936. Two were deployed on the Ardrossan to Belfast night service, following withdrawal of the passenger service on that route with the introduction of the **Royal Scotsman** and **Royal Ulsterman** at Glasgow (Chapter 5). The **Lairdsbank**, which spent all her career on the Heysham to Londonderry service, was briefly transferred to the British & Irish service between Cork and Liverpool as the **Glanmire** in 1963, on which she wore the traditional colours of the City of Cork Steam Packet. These ships were equipped with twin Harland & Wolff-Burmeister & Wain type airless injection engines.

It is noteworthy that the railways were still building steam-engined cargo ships throughout the 1930s. In post-war years, the railways excelled with the world's first cellular container ships, the **Container Venturer** and **Container Enterprise**, which took up service between Belfast and Heysham in 1958. They were built by the Ailsa Shipbuilding Company of Troon, and were equipped with single shafts and an 8-cylinder Polar-Atlas engine. Perhaps the most distinctive class was the neat engine-aft cargo ship series built for Associated Humber Lines between 1958 and 1959, the three **Wakefield**-class ships built by A & J Inglis and the three **Darlington**-class ships built by J Lamont & Company of Port Glasgow. Each was propelled by a Ruston & Hornsby 7-cylinder diesel engine driving a single screw through a reverse/reduction gearbox.

The ultimate cargo ferries were the railway ships **Sea Freightliner I** and **Sea Freightliner II**, which were large and fast cellular container ships built for the Harwich to Zeebrugge route in 1967. The **Brian Boroime** and **Rhodri Mawr** were of similar design and deployed in 1970 between Holyhead and Dublin, at a cost of £1 million per ship and £7 million for two new terminals. The ultimate cattle carrier on this route was the **Slieve Donard**, which was completed as a conventional central island ship in 1959 by the Ailsa Shipbuilding Company and equipped with twin 8-cylinder British Polar engines. It was this ship which provided extensive support in 1964 at Stranraer, carrying passengers' cars alongside the turbine driven vehicular ferry **Caledonian Princess**.

During the 1930s and 1950s, the General Steam Navigation Company pursued the Coast Lines midship accommodation and diesel engines aft design. Other companies such as Ellerman's Wilson Line stayed with steam reciprocating engines, many combined with a low pressure exhaust turbine. Their final conventional build was the **Rapallo**, which dated from 1960, but which was mainly employed on the Prince-Westcott and Ellerman services to the Mediterranean.

The conventional break-bulk cargo and cattle carrier has now long disappeared from British waters. Vehicle ferries had taken over much of the trade by the early 1960s; for example, North Sea Ferries vehicle ferry service to Rotterdam put much of the Associated Humber Lines' vessels out of business. Frank Bustard's Transport Ferry Service had already revolutionised roll-on roll-off traffic to the Continent from Tilbury, and was frightening conventional carriers such as the Belfast Steam Ship Company on the Irish Sea. So great was the threat from the Transport Ferry Service that in the late 1940s the Belfast Steamship Company cried foul over the extremely low charter rates that the new company enjoyed for the use of their converted Tank Landing Craft on commercial services. Perhaps the Chairman and the Board in Belfast should have paid more attention to the roll-on freight concept in the immediate post-war years, so that they too, could have been innovators of the new cargo carrying concept.

The City of Cork Steam Packet's **Glanmire** *(1936), formerly Burns & Laird's* **Lairdsbank***, was one of the very early diesel-powered cargo and cattle-carrying vessels. She is seen here arriving in the River Mersey.*

The 1937-built **Kilkenny** *was a typical Irish Sea cargo and cattle carrier owned by the British and Irish Steam Packet Company. She was broken up at Dalmuir in 1964.*

A later example of the cargo ferry, Belfast Steamship Company's **Ulster Weaver** *(1946) was photographed in the Manchester Ship Canal in 1962. Built as* **Ulster Duchess***, she served also as* **Jersey Coast***, and later* **Kentish Coast***, before being sold to Kuwaiti owners in 1968.*

CHAPTER 10

SOME LITTLE SHIPS

A procession of rather utilitarian diesel driven estuarine ferries came out during the late 1940s and throughout the 1950s. For the most part these were unimaginative in design and lacking in décor, but almost without exception they are remembered by many with affection. The first of these were the sisters, **Southsea** and **Brading**, ordered by the Southern Railway in 1946 and delivered in 1948 to the British Transport Commission, Southern Region at a cost of £160,000 each, for the Portsmouth to Ryde ferry. Short and fat, they had a length of 59 m and a stubby beam of 14.6 m, and as a consequence could accommodate an amazing 1331 passengers in two classes complete with their baggage, and a crew complement of 33. So successful were the pair that a third, the **Shanklin**, came out in 1951.

The three ships were products of William Denny of Dumbarton. The **Southsea** and **Brading** were driven by twin 8-cylinder uni-directional Sulzer engines driving through a reduction gearbox which provided 1475 kW at 375 revolutions per minute, giving the ships a speed of just over 14 knots. The **Shanklin** differed from the earlier pair, as she had direct reversing engines and her shafts were outward turning. The three work horses were essentially a part of the Portsmouth scene throughout the 1950s and 1960s. At speed they tended to dig their heels in, and appeared to plane much as a motor boat does. For all that, and lacking as they did any endearing features such as attractive accommodation, or cosy public spaces, they were valuable money earning units.

*The **Brading** (1948) enters Portsmouth harbour at the completion of a return voyage to Ryde in August 1964.*

First class was aft, third class forward. On the Lower Deck was the first class saloon and refreshment room, with smoke room and bar on the port side and a comfortable lounge on the starboard side; the third class saloon was situated forward of the engine room. There was hold space forward with passenger alleyways either side, which were lined with large windows. A Spar Deck was fitted over the Promenade Deck aft in 1967, and this required stove pipe extensions to the funnels of the older pair, and later lengthening of the funnels, to ensure removal of smuts from the seating area on the new deck. In 1973 the engine room telegraph was dispensed with, to allow direct control of the engines from the bridge.

In 1981 the **Shanklin** was withdrawn and eventually sold to the Firth of Clyde Steam Packet Company for £25,000. Renamed **Prince Ivanhoe**, she was put into service on the Bristol Channel in support of the paddle steamer **Waverley**, but in her first season she struck an object off Port Eynon, was beached and later declared a constructive total loss, with a 20 m gash along her hull, high water later reaching well up the funnel. One passenger died during the stranding, although it took only 40 minutes to evacuate the ship once she had been driven onto the sand. A contemporary account by Alan Brown, a passenger aboard the ship, painted three distinct images:

*The **Shanklin** (1951) comes through the harbour entrance at Portsmouth in March 1968.*

* Looking astern from the Promenade Deck, starboard side, while the ship was drifting off the Port Eynon Point, watching the belting at the stern very gradually getting closer to the surface of the water.
* Standing on the Main Deck at the after end of the engine casing listening to the roar of incoming water.
* Finally sitting on the terrace of the hotel at Horton, after having been brought ashore, and looking across the sand to the stricken ship. Suddenly, and without warning there came the sound of the chime whistle (formerly of the paddle steamer **Glen Usk**), a melodious, melancholy note which gradually faded into silence – the final, dying call of the ill-fated **Prince Ivanhoe**.

The older sisters were retired in 1986. The **Brading** finished up at Pounds shipbreaking yard of Portsmouth where, in November 1995, she caught fire and was destroyed. The **Southsea** remains laid up.

The **Balmoral** was built as a sequel to the pre-war Voith Schneider propelled **Vecta**, for the Southampton, Isle of Wight and South of England Royal Mail Steam Packet Company, in 1949. A little bit more effort was made with this ship than with the Portsmouth ferries, and she was at least given some sheer and a reasonably balanced profile. The **Balmoral** was a product of J I Thornycroft & Company, of Woolston, Southampton, who also built her engines under licence from Newbury-Sirron. The twin 6-cylinder direct-reversing engines were of the airless injection type and developed 450 kW at 300 revolutions per minute, giving her a speed of over 16 knots through conventional shafts and propellers. In service a speed of only 14 knots was generally required. Electricity is provided by two 35 kW Laurence Scott diesel generator units. The original engines served her until replaced in the winter of 2002/2003.

The accommodation on the **Balmoral** consisted of an observation lounge and bar on the Promenade Deck, and a 64 seater dining saloon with small cocktail bar on the Main Deck, surrounded by large square windows. There was room for about 12 cars on the Main Deck aft, loaded via ramps which connect to gates in the bulwarks. On the Lower Deck was a saloon and bar, with seating arranged in three bays on either side of the main staircase leading up to the lounge and a handsome stairway. Much use was made of cream coloured painted bulkheads and upholstered seating. The crew accommodation was forward on the Lower Deck. One nice touch was a viewing area for passengers to see the engines, a reflection of the days of the paddle steamers

Arriving at Barry in June 1969 whilst on charter to P & A Campbell Ltd is the Southampton-registered **Balmoral**, *built twenty years previously.*

that previously maintained the Cowes ferry. The **Balmoral** entered service on 13 December 1949, and has led a charmed existence ever since (see Richard Danielson's account of the **Balmoral** in reference section). Originally the ferry could accommodate 892 passengers but more recently she sails under a Class IV certificate for 800 and a Class III certificate for 691.

The **Balmoral** finished on the Cowes ferry on 15 September 1968. From 1969 she was demise chartered to P & A Campbell and used on a variety of summer excursion services. In 1979 she finally passed into Campbell ownership, and ran in the following year jointly with the Landmark Trust. Sold for £30,000, she moved to Dundee to be used as The Inn on the Quay, but quickly fell into neglect. After five sorry years alongside at Dundee, she was bought by Balmoral Excursions Limited as a running mate and support ship for the paddle steamer **Waverley**. During pre-purchase inspection, her engines started first time, there being just enough compressed air left in the air bottles to complete the ignition procedure. In this, her third life, she has excelled, and few excursionists now remember her as just another mundane Isle of Wight ferry. Having now successfully celebrated her fiftieth anniversary, the **Balmoral** is set to entertain passengers for many seasons yet, although annual maintenance costs will increase as she gets older despite her new engines.

Next came four ships for Wallasey Ferries, one exotic and fanciful, two plain and functional, and one less plain but still functional. These were the first diesel ferries on the Mersey: the cruise ferry **Royal Iris**, the ferries **Egremont** and **Leasowe** and the **Royal Daffodil II**. Like the Portsmouth to Ryde ferries they had exceptionally large breadth to length ratios and were designed specifically for calm estuarine waters. The first was the **Royal Iris**, the largest of all the Mersey ferries, and built with a dual role of ferry and river cruise ship. Built by Denny at Dumbarton, and launched on 8 December 1950, she was equipped with four 6-cylinder Ruston diesels driving two 300 kW constant current generators, which in turn supplied two motors. The electrical equipment was supplied by Metropolitan Vickers Electrical Limited. Output from the motors was 400 kW on three engines for normal ferry duties, and 580 kW with all four engines running should extra speed be required. She could carry 2296 passengers on ferry duties and was limited to 1000 for cruises, not an unremarkable feat for a ship which measured only 1234 gross tons. The main claim to fame for the **Royal Iris** was her outward appearance, complete with a rounded bow and streamlined superstructure; set off in a pale green livery with buff upperworks, she well deserved her Merseyside nickname 'The Electric Iron'.

The Shelter Deck of the **Royal Iris** was fully enclosed and without any camber, making an ideal surface for a dance floor. There was a bar and café on the Lower Deck, situated between the generator room and the motor room. There was also a fish and chip bar complete with ventilation to remove the smells of frying to ventilators on the upper deck. This was removed during a major refit in 1971, when the ferries were transferred to the newly formed Merseyside Passenger Transport Executive. In place of the old fish bar was a new, and considerably up market, steak bar, which was situated on the Main Deck.

The **Leasowe** and **Egremont** came from Phillip & Sons of Dartmouth in 1951. These had twin 8-cylinder Crossley diesels of the direct-reversing two stroke type. The propellers were set wide apart, with twin rudders set inboard to aid manoeuvrability. Passenger accommodation was on three decks, a Sun Deck, Main Deck and Lower Deck. The main saloon was located on the Main Deck, a drab and unimaginative lounge area, with the buffet, bar and smoke room below. On ferry duty some 1472 passengers were carried, but when cruising the complement was reduced to 700.

*The 1951-built **Egremont** in the Mersey in April 1970. In the late 1960s and 1970s, it always fell to this vessel to carry out the schools' voyage from Liverpool, up the Manchester Ship Canal to Pomona Docks at Salford on the Friday, returning the next day to New Brighton via Liverpool Pier Head.*

*The fourth ship was built by James Lamont of Port Glasgow and was launched in 1958 as the **Royal Daffodil II**, losing the suffix in 1968 when the General Steam Navigation Company excursion ship of the same name was withdrawn (Chapter 6). She was photographed off the Princes Landing Stage at Liverpool in March 1967.*

The **Overchurch** of 1962 was photographed when working the ferry service to Birkenhead in April 1970.

In 1974 the **Leasowe** went to Greek waters and the **Egremont** became a club house at Salcombe. As time went on, the **Royal Daffodil** was found to be too large for the ferry run but too small for cruising, and was sold for £55,000 to Greek buyers, who renamed her **Ioulis Keas II** in April 1977. The **Royal Iris** finally left the fleet in 1991, to adopt a static role at Cardiff. They are survived to this day by three younger and smaller sisters built for the Birkenhead Woodside ferry in 1960 and 1962: the **Mountwood**, **Woodchurch** and **Overchurch**. The **Mountwood** was recently restyled for a dual ferry and cruising role as the **Royal Iris of the Mersey** (the name **Royal Iris** still being withheld by her predecessor) and the **Overchurch** as the **Royal Daffodil**.

The ultimate bland design of passenger ferry came out on the Clyde for the Caledonian Steam Packet Company in 1953. These were the four **Maid of Ashton** class vessels. These utilitarian vessels had a Promenade Deck for passenger use aft of the bridge structure, but with no view forward. On the Main Deck were the lounge and tea room, consisting of rows and rows of fixed bus-type seating all facing forward, as if waiting for some talent show to start. Sadly the high bulwarks forward prevented any view through the windows beneath the bridge.

Bland yes, but functional they were too. With capacity for 625 one class passengers, and capable of a speed of 15 knots, they soon became very reliable units on the Clyde. The **Maid of Ashton** was launched on 17 February 1953, and took up service in May, the **Maid of Argyll** and the **Maid of Skelmorlie** followed her into service in June, and **Maid of Cumbrae** in July. Each was equipped with twin 6-cylinder British Polar diesels. The ships survived until the 1970s, the **Maid of Cumbrae** receiving a car ramp to a cut away Main Deck aft in 1973. The **Maid of Ashton** moved to the Victoria Embankment in London in 1973, where she is still in use in a static role. The other three were sold for further service in the Mediterranean; the **Maid of Argyll** and **Maid of Skelmorlie** were still in active service in 2001.

The **Maid of Ashton** (1953) arrives at Gourock with a full load of passengers in July 1969.

Three more ferries were planned for the Caledonian Steam Packet Company, this time with side loading facilities for cars. In the event they appeared as the "ABC" car and passenger ferries with the names **Arran**, **Bute** and **Cowal**. The **Arran** opened the Dunoon to Gourock car ferry service in January 1954, and was joined in April by the **Cowal** (the **Cowal** was the first Caledonian Steam Packet Company ship to have radar), and the **Bute** followed in September. Between them they maintained the Rothesay and Gourock services. As built, they could carry 605 passengers and 26 cars, the latter loaded by means of a side ramp to a hoist. The after part of the small car deck could be accessed via a hold, and there were derricks and samson posts to assist cargo handling. The passenger accommodation was forward of this on two decks. In 1959 the cargo handling gear was removed, and the hold was plated over to provide room for an additional ten cars.

The ABC ferries were equipped with similar 6-cylinder British Polar engines to the four Maids, only the bore and stroke were considerably larger. As such they could manage a handsome 15 knots in service. In 1972, the **Arran** was rebuilt at a cost of £100,000 as a stern loading ferry for use on the West Loch Tarbert to Islay service. She was withdrawn in 1979, two years after the **Bute** had finished on the Clyde and one year after the **Cowal** had retired to the James Watt Dock for the last time. The **Arran** was never used again, and was eventually broken up in Manchester in 1993. Her sisters went to Greece, but again saw no further service, and were scrapped in 1983/84.

*Seagulls attend the arrival of the **Bute** (1954) at Rothesay, the main town on the island after which she was named, in July 1967.*

A larger development of the same theme followed from the Ailsa shipyard in Troon in 1957. This was the **Glen Sannox**, which was designed for the Ardrossan (Fairlie in winter) to Brodick route, and was given accommodation for 1100 passengers and side loading hoists for 60 cars or equivalent commercial vehicles and cargo. She cost about £500,000 to build. A major departure from the previous seven diesel ships in the fleet was her Sulzer diesels, which were twin 8-cylinder engines with a bore of 400 mm and a stroke of 500 mm. These provided the ship with a service speed of 18 knots. Unlike the ABC ships which had electric hoists, the hoist on the **Glen Sannox** was hydraulic. Although the hoist was more powerful than those of her smaller consorts, it was much slower in operation and the **Glen Sannox** needed every bit of her fast speed to catch up on her schedule when heavily loaded. A stern ramp was fitted in 1970, and the **Glen Sannox** was used on a variety of routes, including services out of Oban, until sold in 1989 for further service in the Middle East.

*Seagulls are once again prominent as the 1957-built **Glen Sannox** approaches the harbour at Ardrossan upon arrival from Brodick on 16 July 1969. At this date, she stiill sported the buff funnel colour and badge of the Caledonian Steam Packet Company.*

A number of small second generation turntable ferries were also built for service on the Skye ferry for the Caledonian Steam Packet Company. Replacing the one-and two-car capacity ferries described in Chapter 2, and now with an enlarged slipway at both terminals, the larger vessels **Portree**, **Broadford**, **Lochalsh** and **Kyleakin** were delivered by Denny and the Ailsa Shipbuilding Company, between 1951 and 1960. They each had twin 4-cylinder Gleniffer diesel units which gave them a speed of between $8\frac{1}{2}$ and $9\frac{1}{2}$ knots. These ships could carry between four and six cars, and up to 100 passengers, on the ten minute crossing between Kyle of Lochalsh and Kyleakin. Subsequent ferries for the route were side or end loading.

Other small estuarine car and passenger ferries built in the 1950s were the **Freshwater**, built for the railway's Lymington to Yarmouth service and the **Carisbrooke Castle** for the Southampton, Isle of Wight and South of England Royal Mail Steam Packet Company. The **Freshwater**, like the pre-war **Lymington** (Chapter 6), had twin Crossley diesels connected to Voith Schneider units, and replaced the elderly paddle steamer of the same name. Replacement car ferries for the Portsmouth station were not delivered until 1961, when the **Fishbourne** and **Camber Queen** displaced the three prototype ferries **Fishbourne**, **Wootton** and **Hilsea** (described in Chapter 2)

It may be a November day in 1969 but the sun is clearly shining as the **Freshwater** (1959) approaches Yarmouth pier on the Isle of Wight.

The **Osborne Castle** of 1962 arrives at Southampton in March 1968.

The **Carisbrooke Castle** was built by J I Thornycroft in 1959, and was the first of a series of four similar vessels. A highly innovative design, she cost just over £300,000 to build. She had twin 8-cylinder Crossley diesel engines, which gave her a service speed of 14 knots. The **Carisbrooke Castle** could accommodate up to 40 cars loaded over a bow ramp, or through side doors, and 433 passengers (1200 passengers with an empty vehicle deck). She had a large observation lounge and saloon on the Promenade Deck, there was also a buffet bar and a ladies' room. Successors in this same class were the **Osborne Castle**, **Cowes Castle** and **Norris Castle**.

The Southampton-based tug/tender **Gatcombe** (1960) heads up Southampton Water in October 1967.

In addition there were two diesel driven tug-tenders in the Southampton 'Red Funnel' fleet, most other such vessels having been steam driven. The **Calshot/Galway Bay**, built in 1930, was converted only at a late stage in her career to diesel, but there were also the diesel driven Cork tenders **Blarna** and **Cill Airne** dating from 1961 and 1962 respectively. The two Southampton-based diesel tug-tenders were the **Gatcombe** which was built in 1960, and had a gross tonnage of 475, and the **Calshot**, which was built in 1964, and had a gross tonnage of 494. The latter was the last surviving tug-tender in the UK when she was sold for further service overseas in 1986.

An earlier vehicle ferry with the name **Norris Castle** had been converted for the Southampton company from a Landing Craft Tank by Thornycroft in 1948. She was equipped with twin 6-cylinder Davey Paxman diesel engines, but could only manage 11 knots. Cars and commercial vehicles were loaded either over a bow ramp or via side ports in the bulwarks. Loading was via a pontoon and bridge at Southampton, built from parts of one of the former war time Mulberry Harbours, and over a concrete slipway at East Cowes. The **Norris Castle** also carried much of the heavy plant directly up the River Medina for the island's electricity and gas works situated at Kingston. She was retired in 1962, although she had been extensively rebuilt only two years earlier, and later saw service in the Mediterranean.

In 1949, John Hall, who had previously operated the excursion ship **Royal Lady** during 1947 (Chapter 6), put forward plans to run a new vehicle ferry service across the Forth between Granton and Burntisland. This was despite the Forth Road Bridge Act which had been passed by Parliament only two years previously. A public company, Forth Ferries Limited was created, and four Landing Craft Tank were brought round from lay-up at Portsmouth. Conversion took place on the Clyde, and included the fitting of bilge keels, and provision of side loading doors to suit the slipways. Conversion was slow, and the first vessel, the **Bonnie Prince Charlie**, only ran trials at the end of June 1950. Formerly the **LCT 4-673**, the **Bonnie Prince Charlie** now had accommodation for up to forty cars and passenger facilities that included a tea lounge, cocktail bar and a sheltered Boat Deck. The **LCT 893** became the **Flora Macdonald** and the **LCT 1048** became the **Glenfinnan**. The fourth conversion, the **Eriskay**, was ready at Granton in January 1951, but the ferry service did not start until April.

Although the summer traffic was above expectations, the winter returns were poor. Given the cost of the delayed start to the service and mounting losses, the company was forced to cease trading in December 1952. The four ships lay at Leith until 1954, when they were towed out to India for use as ore carriers; they received the exotic names **Surendra**, **Prapida**, **Hemelata** and **Pracaxa**.

*The **Jersey Queen** (1944), formerly the **Rochester Queen** and **Commodore Queen**, at Poole in June 1974.*

A number of other interesting small diesel powered passenger vessels were converted from military use in post war years. One of these was the New Medway Steam Packet Company's excursion ship **Rochester Queen**, which was built in1944 as **LCG(M) 181**; another was the **Sark Coast** of the Coast Lines' fleet which was built in 1945 as **LCG (M) 196**. Both ships were former Landing Craft (Guns), and were converted by Bolsons of Poole for civilian use in 1948. As these landing craft were originally fitted with fairly large guns, there was a need to ballast them to obtain sufficient stability to cater for the gun's weight, as well as the recoil from a shot fired broadside. For this, the ships had a large floodable double bottom, which also provided them with an additional safety factor in civilian life. Given twin Paxman engines, there was saloon accommodation on the Lower Deck, and a central deckhouse containing a lounge. The original transom stern was rounded off, and the bulwarks had an attractive sheer to them. Sold in 1955 to German owners, the **Rochester Queen** came back to the British registry in 1961 as the **Commodore Queen**, and later the **Jersey Queen**, before being sold for use as a survey ship off West Africa. The **Sark Coast** was chartered to British Channel Islands Shipping (Guernsey) Limited, and sold on in 1954 to owners in Martinique. An American assault craft was converted for excursion use at Brighton in 1950, and was given the name **Regency Belle**. After three seasons she was sold to the Torbay Cruising Company, becoming a popular attraction in South Devon.

David MacBrayne had the 1942 built former wooden inshore minesweeper **Loch Arkaig** rebuilt for the Mallaig and Kyle of Lochalsh to Portree service, with a summer certificate for 234 passengers. This little ship was given twin 4-cylinder engines, built by Bergius, on her conversion for civilian use in 1959. She transferred to the Rhum, Eigg, Muck and Canna service when a smaller vessel, the **Loch Eynort**, was converted for the service in 1961. This little vessel was formerly the Commissioners of Irish Lights' pilot boat **Valonia**, was built in 1947 with twin 4-cylinder Crossley engines and was capable of just over 8 knots. The **Loch Eynort** could accommodate 150 passengers. The **Loch Arkaig** sank in Mallaig Harbour in 1979, but was raised and later served Spanish owners for a further six years, before ending her career by sinking again. The **Loch Eynort** left Scotland in 1970, and was later used as the **Skellig** for film work.

*The diminutive **Loch Eynort**, dating from 1947, approaches the pier at Portree, Isle of Skye, in windy conditions during August 1964.*

Perhaps the most attractive conversion of a military vessel was that of the **Island Commodore**. Laid down in 1942 as a torpedo recovery vessel, the **TRV 2** was only completed in 1946, and was then converted for passenger and cargo duties on acquisition by the Commodore Shipping Company Limited, later transferring to the Alderney and Sark Shipping Company. She had a licence to carry 144 passengers. In 1970 she became the **Ile de Serk**, when she was bought by the Isle of Sark Shipping Company. She completed her last trip between Guernsey and Sark on 20 November 1983, when she was seen away from her namesake isle with a farewell party.

*Formerly a torpedo recovery vessel, the little **Ile de Serk** (1942 - 1946) is seen at St Peter Port, Guernsey, on 8 June 1974.*

There were about twenty Fairmile Type B launches converted for excursion use. Given diesel engines instead of their military petrol engines, they could manage 12 knots, and, with a gross tonnage typically of about 120, they had a passenger complement of between 200 and 250. Some of these small vessels remained in service throughout the 1990s, having been a common sight at the majority of English seaside resorts for many years.

One of the oddest converted passenger craft was the **Wimaisia**, a diesel electric screw-driven former tug, the **Duchess of Abercorn**, which in her new role plied slowly down the Clyde to Campbeltown every other day in 1948. Later she served as the Liverpool fire-boat **William Gregson**.

However, the last newbuildings of the 1950s were the small Tilbury to Gravesend, passenger-only ferries **Rose**, **Edith** and **Catherine**. They were built at Southampton by White's Shipyard and, though small, were of an advanced design. Rapid turnround was helped by three hydraulically operated passenger gangways installed along each side, and propulsion comprised a single Voith Schneider unit coupled to a 6-cylinder Lister Blackstone engine. Although the mass transit of commuters across this short stretch of river did not persist, all three ships pursued useful second careers: the **Rose** became the excursion ship **Keppel** on the Clyde and is presently working as a harbour tour boat in Valletta's Grand Harbour, the **Catherine** became an excursion vessel on the Tyne, and the **Edith** has been used for many years as a Thames house boat.

A notable exception to the bland design of small ferries during the 1950s was the Irish **Naom Éanna**. The **Naom Éanna** was built by the Liffey Dockyard in 1958 for the nationalised transport undertaking Coras Iompair Eireann. She was equipped with a single 6-cylinder Bollinder type British Polar engine which drove the shaft via gearing. She served the Aran Islands out of Galway with a certificate for 312 passengers, including twelve berths, and a single hold forward. Although she called at a pier at Kilronan on Inishmore, visits to Inishmann and Inishere islands were serviced by canvas-sided currachs, each with three pairs of oars, rowing out to the ship, with cattle swimming behind to be lifted aboard in a sling. The **Naom Éanna** made two or three runs to the islands each week at a steady and determined 10 knots, and was eventually retired at the age of 30. A good sea boat of only 483 tons gross, her appearance was stocky and solid. There might only have been a few scheduled trips missed because of the weather, but there were many passengers that stood at the stern rail wishing they had not had such a big Irish fried breakfast before setting out! She remains in static use in Dublin.

CHAPTER 11

SINGLE AND TWIN SCREW CLASSIC FERRIES

Although the 1950s had been host to a stream of bland and unimaginative coastal and estuarine ferries (Chapter 10), it was also the time when an attractive series of larger classic passenger and cargo diesel ferries evolved. The decade started with the delivery of the **St Ninian** by the Robb Caledon shipyard of Dundee to the North of Scotland, Orkney and Shetland Shipping Company Limited in 1950. The largest ship in the fleet at that time, the **St Ninian** was nevertheless of modest proportions by today's standards, with a gross tonnage of only 2242, and a reputation of being very lively in a rough sea. The decade ended with the delivery of the ultimate passenger and cargo ferry, the **St Clair**, to the same owners in 1960.

The **St Ninian** had comfortable cabin accommodation for 200 passengers. The cabins were characterised by polished brass bunk fittings typical of an earlier era. The dining saloon tables were always immaculately laid with the company's best silver and crockery. There was a dark wood panelled smoke room and bar, and a more airy lounge which faced forward. In additional to the cabin accommodation, the **St Ninian** was certified to carry up to 340 deck passengers, for whom ample seating was available, but little of which, it seems, had been designed with the comfort of the overnight passenger in mind. The ship also boasted considerable cargo space, with holds forward and aft of the accommodation island, each served by electric derricks.

*The **St Ninian** (1950) leaving the quay at Kirkwall in August 1968.*

The **St Ninian** was equipped with twin 8-cylinder direct-reversing British Polar engines which gave her a handsome speed of 15 knots. She also had an extremely noisy Ruston generator unit for domestic and auxiliary power. The **St Ninian** commenced her maiden voyage on the Leith, Aberdeen, Kirkwall and Lerwick route on 5 June 1950, and settled to a weekly routine round trip. This was always popular with tourists who could combine the voyage with a stop over in one or more of the company hotels on the islands. For the most part, she left Leith on Monday evening and returned from Lerwick at 2100 or 2200 hours on Thursday, returning to Leith on Saturday night.

Closure of the Leith service in January 1971 was followed by six weeks relief on the direct Aberdeen to Lerwick route, finishing at Aberdeen on 28 February. The ship was bought for service in Canada, but after extensive lay up in Nova Scotia, ended her days as the Galapagos Islands ferry from Ecuador under the name **Buccaneer**.

A smaller vessel was built by Hall, Russell & Company of Aberdeen for the Scrabster to Stromness service of the North Company. This was the **St Ola**, completed in 1951 with a modest gross tonnage of only 750. She traversed the Pentland Firth at just over 12 knots, driven by a single shaft connected to a 7-cylinder direct-reversing British Polar engine, occasionally diverting though Scapa Flow when the weather was bad. The engines of the pre-war **Earl of Zetland**, the **St Ninian**, the **St Clement** (Chapter 9) and the **St Ola** all had the same bore of 340 mm and stroke of 570 mm, and to a large extent engine parts were interchangeable between them.

*The **St Ola** of 1951 goes astern from her berth at Stromness, Orkney, in August 1968.*

The **St Ola** was a marvellous sea boat. Standing aft watching the horizon appear and disappear over the bridge housing off the high cliffs of Hoy was a memorable experience, although not one that was conducive to enjoying her excellent catering facilities. As a day passenger ship, the **St Ola** could carry 359 passengers in summer and 339 in winter; she could also carry up to 30 cars in her single forward hold and strapped down on the forward deck, each vehicle laboriously loaded and unloaded with the ship's own derrick. In her first season on the route, 900 cars were carried, and this quickly increased to over 2000 per year, becoming an impossible 9500 by 1975, when she was replaced by a car ferry of the same name. A single round trip was normally advertised, but a double trip was made at peak times.

In her early years, the **St Ola** also undertook a number of excursion services to Scapa and to view the Old Man of Hoy. The **St Ola** also relieved the **Earl of Zetland** (Chapter 4), and in many ways the **Earl of Zetland** was the natural predecessor of the **St Ola**. For winter overhaul each year, the **St Ola** was herself relieved by the cargo vessel **St Clement** (Chapter 9), and it was the **St Clement**, which, in summer, assisted with heavy car traffic on the route.

The next of the larger cross channel diesel ferries to be built was the magnificent **Irish Coast**, which was launched at Belfast on 8 May 1952 by the wife of the Chairman of Coast Lines. She cost £0.8 million. This was a ship which was distinguished in a number of ways, but not least in that she was designed for summer and autumn service on the Glasgow to Dublin route, and to spend the winter as the relief vessel for other Irish Sea services. Her maiden voyage, for example, took place on 1 November 1952 from Liverpool to Belfast as relief for the **Ulster Prince** (see Chapter 5). That the **Irish Coast** was the most luxuriously appointed vessel of them all seems quite odd. That she was basically constructed around the design of the **Ulster Monarch**, which dated from the late 1920s, and designed without any cognisance of the roll-on/roll-off concept which was now successfully being developed out of Preston by the Atlantic Steam Navigation Company, seems even odder. That being so, the **Irish Coast** was an investment that Coast Lines could ill afford.

The saving grace for Coast Lines was that they had at least adopted the diesel engine at an early stage. This was in stark contrast to the staid British Railways Board, which was yet to order three steam turbine driven Duke-class vessels for the Heysham to Belfast route, and which stayed loyal to steam rather than diesel well into the 1960s. The main engines of the **Irish Coast** were described in a supplement to the *Journal of Commerce* in 1952 as:

"Main machinery of the **Irish Coast** consists of two trunk-type two-cycle airless-injection Harland-B&W oil engines of the builder's latest design. Each engine has 10 cylinders 500 mm diameter by 900 mm stroke and develops the necessary power at about 155 revolutions per minute. The engines are reversing type, coupled direct to the propelling shaft."

The need for a relief vessel stemmed from the absence of each of the Coast Lines Group's passenger vessels from the Irish Sea for up to one month each winter for overhaul. This detailed care over the maintenance of the ships certainly contributed to their longevity, although this was not uncommon with shipowners at that time, keen to keep depreciation to a minimum.

The **Irish Coast**, *dating from 1951, leaves her berth at Glasgow's Broomielaw Quay in July 1967.*

The *Irish Coast* was distinguished in that she carried the colours of her parent company throughout her career on the Irish Sea – the only cross-channel ship to proudly wear the black funnel and white chevron of Coast Lines.

The saloon class passenger accommodation was decorated in pale African hardwoods which contrasted with dark red leather upholstery. A total of 246 saloon passengers were accommodated with berths in single and double cabins, one four berth family cabin and two twin berth state rooms. An additional 554 unberthed saloon class passengers could be carried in summer, although the total winter passenger complement was only 750 for both saloon and second class. The A Deck lounge featured an authentic log fire in a marble fireplace; the Promenade Deck smoking room was adorned in chestnut wood with coral coloured leather seating, and there was even a cocktail bar recessed into the after part of the funnel on the Sun Deck (!) in which the bulkheads were draped with nineteenth century prints. The smoking room was designed as a male-only preserve, but the Irish ladies lost no time in bringing it into the modern era as a room for all to enjoy! The whole décor on the ship was much along the principle of the pre-war luxury liners.

The second class accommodation aboard the *Irish Coast* comprised two and four berth cabins for 146 passengers and dormitories for men and women. Her summer passenger certificate allowed her to carry an additional 254 unberthed steerage passengers. Much improved on earlier Coast Lines' vessels, the steerage accommodation remained at the stern of the ship (hence the name steerage, which was in fact Third Class accommodation). Some thought that this was an unhealthy distance from the lifeboats. This safety problem had earlier been remedied in the design of the *Cambria* and *Hibernia* for the railways (Chapter 8), who moved the steerage class accommodation into the centre island away from the poop, but the issue was ignored by the Coast Lines' management. In addition, the *Irish Coast* offered permanent stalls for 358 cattle and eight horses in the 'tween decks, and the No. 2 hold was able to accommodate up to 50 cars.

On her early morning arrival at Liverpool, the **Scottish Coast** (1957) goes astern through Princes Half Tide Dock towards her berth in Princes Dock in May 1967.

Only four years later Coast Lines surprisingly ordered a consort for the *Irish Coast*. This was the even more majestic *Scottish Coast*. Her funnel was originally adorned in the red and black of the Belfast Steamship Company. The *Scottish Coast* later wore the red, dusty blue and black colours of Burns and Laird Lines, but she never wore that of her owners, Coast Lines, even though their chevron was outlined in rivets in the funnel from the outset. Built also by Harland & Wolff, the cost this time had risen to £1.1 million, more than the combined cost of the *Ulster Monarch* and her two sisters twenty seven years earlier. The new ship was launched on 21 August 1956 by the wife of the Northern Ireland Minister of Commerce, Lady Glentoran.

The *Scottish Coast* was the thirteenth and last member of the *Ulster Monarch* class – some observers claiming a class of fifteen with the Holyhead based railway ships *Cambria* and *Hibernia* deriving also from this same design. Needless to say, the original design of the *Ulster Monarch*-class had certainly been justified time and again. There were slight differences in the accommodation between the last two ships of the class. For example, the *Scottish Coast* carried a Highland theme in the 82-seater saloon restaurant, and berthed slightly different numbers in saloon (first) and third class than did the *Irish Coast*. Like her consort, the new ship also served on relief duties; her maiden voyage on 4 March 1957 allowed the *Ulster Monarch* to retire to Belfast for upgrading and maintenance.

The new *Scottish Coast* displaced the *Irish Coast* from the Glasgow to Dublin route in August 1957. Thereafter the *Irish Coast* maintained the summer only Ardrossan to Belfast day service, allowing the elderly turbine steamer *Lairds Isle* to retire. From 1965 onwards, the *Irish Coast* interchanged with the *Scottish Coast* on the Glasgow to Dublin route until the Ardrossan day route was withdrawn in 1968. The services of the *Irish Coast* then became surplus to requirements and she was laid up for sale in Morpeth Dock, Birkenhead, on 11 April, after finishing with a short stint on the Glasgow to Belfast service. She then joined the Epirotiki fleet of Greek flag cruise vessels in the eastern Mediterranean under a variety of names of Greek heroes and gods. Later resold to the Philippines, and given the name *Regency*, she was wrecked during a hurricane in October 1989.

From the summer of 1965 onwards, the **Scottish Coast** operated out of Ardrossan for which route a hoist was placed in the forward deck to allow side loading of up to 25 cars. At the end of the 1969 summer season, the **Scottish Coast** was laid up in Morpeth Branch Dock in Birkenhead, later also to become a Greek flag cruise ship, initially under the name **Galaxias**. She was scrapped in 2002 as the Cypriot **Princess Amorosa**; the very last of the **Ulster Monarch** class.

The last classic passenger and cargo ferry to be commissioned by David MacBrayne Limited, was the **Claymore**. She was launched from Denny's yard at Dumbarton on 10 March 1955, and her design broadly followed that of the postwar-built **Loch Seaforth** (Chapter 8). The new ship was 15 m shorter in length and 0.5 m shorter in the beam but had only a slightly lower gross tonnage of 1024. She was equipped with two 8-cylinder airless injection engines built by Denny under licence from Sulzer, each with a bore of 360 mm and a stroke of 600 mm. Her service speed was 12 knots.

The passenger accommodation for 494 included some overnight berths. These comprised 6 de-luxe state rooms, 8 single and 5 double cabins in first class, and 7 two-berth cubicles separated by partitions in second class. The **Claymore** had a first class observation lounge and bar on the Promenade Deck as well as a second class lounge; the respective dining saloons were on the Main Deck. The first class public rooms featured highland and coastal birds arranged in wood veneer panels, and the first class dining saloon doors comprised glass panels engraved with the MacBrayne Highlander (which logo also appeared on the bow of the vessel). The **Claymore** had twin holds forward, which were served by an electrically operated derrick. There was capacity for about 100 tonnes of cargo including up to 11 cars and there were moveable stalls for 26 cattle.

*The 1955-built **Claymore** arrives at Oban in the summer of 1967.*

Placed on her design route out of Oban to Coll, Tiree and the outer isles, the new ship displaced the elderly **Lochearn** (see Chapter 4). As such, the **Claymore** represented the very first of the second generation UK diesel ferries. With three trips per week to the islands, departing Oban at 0700 hours on Monday, Wednesday and Friday, and returning at noon the next day, the **Claymore** was able to undertake some excursion work on selected summer afternoons during her turnaround at Oban. She led an uneventful life, occasionally carrying out relief duties for the **Loch Seaforth**, and only became newsworthy when she collided with the coaster **Druid** off Tobermory. Even that incident only put the **Claymore** out of service for a week whilst repairs were effected at Greenock. She was eventually sold out of the fleet in 1976, and started a new and successful second career as a day cruise ship between the Greek islands. As the **City of Hydra**, she was laid up at Elefsis in 1993, following the collapse of her owners, Cycladic Cruises, and eventually sank at her moorings in 2000, later to be recovered and scrapped.

Very much a first generation diesel ferry was the **Scillonian**, which was built by J I Thornycroft, of Southampton. She replaced the 1927-built vessel of the same name, which had been equipped with triple expansion steam reciprocating machinery. The new **Scillonian** was ordered in April 1953 by the Isles of Scilly Steamship Company, launched in November 1955 and then undertook her maiden voyage in March 1956. She was powered by twin 6-cylinder Ruston and Hornsby four stroke diesels, which gave her a service speed of over 15 knots, compared with her predecessor, which could only maintain 12 knots. The cost of the new ship was £250,000.

As a day passenger and cargo ship she could accommodate 500 passengers, as well as all the provisions and supplies for the islands in her two forward holds. There was a central, large, wood-panelled and rather dark lounge on the Main Deck, and there was also a small bar and cafeteria. The **Scillonian** spent a largely uneventful life on the Scilly run, occasionally having berthing difficulties in exceptional weather. She was nevertheless an excellent, albeit a lively sea boat. Her tendency to roll in rough weather was not helped by her draught, which was designed for the shallow waters at St Mary's.

A consort, the **Queen of the Isles**, was built by Charles Hill of Bristol at a cost of £180,000, and was launched in November 1965. Again, twin Ruston and Hornsby diesels were used, though of slightly less power, the resultant service speed was 13.5 knots, but with a high fuel consumption of 120 litres per hour. A smaller vessel with a gross tonnage of only 515, she could carry 300 passengers in spacious and airy accommodation, and had a capacity for 125 tonnes of cargo. The **Queen of the Isles** was a rather stubby looking vessel, and was designed with a view to lengthening should trade conditions ever require. Her primary role, however, was to service the house building boom then taking place in the Scillies, and to act as relief for the **Scillonian** in winter. Her career was a short one; her services were curtailed by the introduction of restrictions in house building on the islands in the mid-1960s, coupled with the opening of the Penzance heliport in 1964 and the introduction of large capacity Sikorski helicopters on the service to the islands.

On charter to P & A Campbell in the summer of 1969, the **Queen of the Isles** (1965) goes astern off Shanklin Pier, Isle of Wight.

A number of charters helped pay her way, including one to P & A Campbell for North Wales excursions in 1968 and on the south coast and Thames in 1969. The **Queen of the Isles** even had a brief charter in spring 1970 to Norwest Hovercraft for their Fleetwood to Douglas route, awaiting the arrival of the **Norwest Laird**, ex-**Lochiel** (Chapter 4). It was not surprising when later that year, she was bought by the Overseas Development Agency (now the UK Department for International Development) for use by the Tonga Shipping Agency in 1970. She subsequently operated under a variety of names, ending up on a reef near Honiara during Cyclone Justin in 1997.

The **Scillonian** was replaced by the very last classic passenger and cargo ship to be built for UK waters, the **Scillonian III**, in 1977. The new ship has twin Mirrlees Blackstone 8-cylinder reverse-reduction geared engines, which provide a speed of 15 knots. The old **Scillonian** was renamed **Devonia**, and was placed on excursions on the Thames by P & A Campbell, who had decided to buy her for £150,000, but it was quickly realised that she was not to be a success in this role. Her limited passenger accommodation did not suit her to the role of excursion ship, although she was again used the following year in the Bristol Channel.

Built in 1956 as **Scillonian**, the final work in the UK for this vessel saw her many miles from the area which she was built to serve. As **Syllingar**, she was photographed leaving Invergordon on 27 June 1985.

She was then sold to J G & M M Thompson for £90,000, for use between Torquay and the Channel Islands as the **Devoniun** (Campbell's insisted they should retain the name **Devonia** and the obvious alternative **Devonian** was already in use) and later between Invergordon and the Orkney Islands as the **Syllingar** (the Norse name for the Scillies), finishing in August 1985. As such, she still carried a framed message of goodwill under a portrait photograph of former Prime Minister Harold Wilson, who had a holiday cottage on the Scillies and who had regularly travelled on the ship. By 1986 her Scottish owners had been forced into liquidation, and the **Syllingar** sailed to Piraeus under the Greek flag as the **Remvi**, to be extensively rebuilt for cruising.

The new **Scillonian III** was built by Appledore Shipbuilders in North Devon and was in service by May 1977. She carries a crew of 19 and is licensed for the carriage of 600 passengers on a Class IIA certificate as well as general cargo, the latter in two forward holds separated by an electrically operated derrick. The passenger lounges and the cafeteria are spacious, and there is plenty of deck space for passengers to enjoy the passing scenery. Catering is simple but adequate, and orders are taken on the outward morning trip for picnics to enjoy whilst visiting the islands. Twin diesels drive the ship at 15 knots via 3: 1 reduction gearing. The **Scillonian III** remains in service, although plans are now in hand to replace her with a new vessel.

A most attractive pair of motor ships were built by Brooke Marine Limited of Lowestoft for Associated Humber Lines' overnight Hull to Rotterdam service. The first, the **Bolton Abbey**, began her commercial career in June 1958, replacing the elderly steam reciprocating engined **Bury**, which had been built for the Great Central Railway in 1910. The new ship was followed into service in January 1959 by the **Melrose Abbey**, which replaced her namesake of 1929 vintage. The new ships were too big for the Humber Dock, so the **Bolton Abbey** had to use the Albert and William Wright Dock until new facilities at Riverside Quay were opened just in time for the arrival of her sister. At the same time the Rotterdam terminal also switched from the Parkhaven to Prinses Beatrixhaven.

The new ships were equipped with twin 8-cylinder Ruston and Hornsby engines, which produced a combined power of 3100 kW, to provide a service speed of just over 15 knots via single reduction forward and astern gearing. The ships were essentially break-bulk cargo ships with two large holds, which were served by three pairs of derricks for cargo handling. The superstructure was aft, with accommodation on two decks for 80 passengers in one class (increased to 88 in 1962 by doubling up 8 single berth cabins), as well as the crew of 31, which included 12 staff dedicated to the catering department. Although the ships only carried about half the number of passengers that their predecessors had done, they were faster and were capable of making the journey in 13$\frac{1}{2}$ rather than 17$\frac{1}{2}$ hours.

The **Melrose Abbey**, *of 1958, and sister ship* **Bolton Abbey**, *were popular with passengers. The former vessel moves off the Riverside Quay at Hull and begins her voyage down the Humber after her early evening departure in August 1967.*

The passenger accommodation comprised a foyer with shop, a lounge bar which overlooked the forward deck, and several cabins (including a de luxe suite) situated on A Deck. The dining room was on B Deck directly beneath the lounge, and there was further cabin accommodation, also on B Deck. Catering was homely, but to a high standard, served by a team of stewards and a stewardess. Round-trip cruises were always popular, as well as cheap, at £9 10p two-night return (in 1969), inclusive of a trip round the bulb fields.

During the winter 1968/69 the pair were sent to Smiths Dock at North Shields for conversion to unit loading of containers and lengthening by 16 m. During the conversion, the cargo handling gear was removed, although the passenger accommodation remained unchanged. By 1971, rival North Sea Ferries (Chapter 12) were beginning to steal much of the traffic on offer, and considerable losses led to the rapid closure of the service. The last return trip was that of the **Melrose Abbey**, which left Hull on 29 November 1971, and returned from Rotterdam two days later. The pair were sold to a Greek company for £135,000; the **Melrose Abbey** was resold for demolition in 1980, her sister was sold on for use in the oil industry in 1974, and in 1983 was also scrapped.

The very last overnight passenger and cargo ferry built for UK service was the **St Clair**. She was launched from the Ailsa Shipyard at Troon on 29 February 1960, having been designed specifically for the Aberdeen to Lerwick service of the North of Scotland, Orkney & Shetland Shipping Company. She was a substantial vessel with three holds and a certificate for 500 passengers. The **St Clair** was equipped with a single 8-

*The **St Clair** (1960) leaves Aberdeen harbour for her overnight voyage to Shetland on 24 August 1970.*

cylinder Sulzer diesel, which was connected to the shaft via reduction reversing gears and which could be controlled directly from the bridge. The service speed of the ship was 13 knots, and her gross tonnage was 3302. She was fitted with Denny-Brown stabilizers when built; alas these could only be deployed once clear of the harbour entrance at Aberdeen, by which point the prevailing swell had often already cleared the saloon tables. John Stevenson, former relief engineer on many of the North Company vessels, recalls:

"The swell as you passed through the piers even on a relatively calm day could be unbelievably fierce. Those passengers who were not regulars, despite warnings from the stewards, would settle down to have dinner at six o'clock as the vessel was sailing. Twenty minutes later they were wishing that they hadn't been so hasty!"

The passenger accommodation on the **St Clair** was memorably spacious, with public rooms and cabins distributed across four separate decks. There was much use of dark wood panelling, which tended to inhibit the feeling of spaciousness, but nevertheless her lounge, bar and smoke room, and dining saloon were attractive and well appointed. Passengers had access to the Bridge Deck and the Boat Deck, from which the phosphorescent wake of the ship could be viewed in the moonlight, or land watched from afar in summer daylight in the 'wee hours'. Most of the cabin accommodation was on the Main Deck and Lower Deck.

The only departures from the Lerwick route were occasional deputising visits to the Liverpool to Belfast service covering for the overhaul period. She was relatively slow on this service and could only accommodate 29 craned-on cars. The last trip of the **St Clair** (then renamed **St Clair II** to relieve her name for her roll-on/roll-off successor) on the Lerwick service was outward on the 9 June 1977 returning two mornings later to Aberdeen. Her send off from Lerwick included flares from the Coastguards, sirens and whistles, and that last night aboard the ferry all drinks in the bar were free. After a short period of lay up, and still only a young ship at the age of 17, she went to Kuwait owners under the new name of **Al Khairat**.

One further inter island ferry service deserves mention in the context of last of the classic ships, that of the Orkney Islands Shipping Company. The company was formed in1960 as a Government-owned successor to the Orkney Steam Navigation Company, created to finance a new building to replace the elderly steamer **Earl Thorfinn**. The new ship was the attractive little vessel **Orcadia**, which was delivered from Hall, Russell at Aberdeen in June 1962, and which originally carried the port of Leith, and not Kirkwall, on her stern, reflecting her ownership by the Secretary of State for Scotland. She was equipped with a single British Polar turbo-charged engine, which in later years became expensive to maintain, as spares were difficult to obtain. The running mate for the new **Orcadia** on the North Isles routes was the **Earl Sigurd**, a compatriot of the venerable **Earl Thorfinn**, which the new ship replaced. However, in 1969 the **Islander**, with a certificate for just 12 passengers replaced the other steamer. The **Islander** had twin Paxman V8 engines connected to a single variable pitch propeller. One of the engines was always kept running in port to generate power for cargo handling. The original engines, however, proved troublesome and were replaced in 1980 with a pair of in-line Deutz engines.

The **Orcadia** could carry 358 passengers on her short inter-island voyages, and she also undertook excursion work and special sailings to suit social gatherings such as local shows and games. She also did occasional charters on the Stromness to Scrabster route for P&O (who by then had taken over the former North Company). The passenger accommodation centred on the lounge and buffet beneath the Bridge on the Main Deck. Cargo was loaded by the ship's derrick, and could include cars, small unitised containers, agricultural machinery and materials, as well as livestock. Replaced by new roll-on/roll-off vessels in 1990, the **Orcadia** was sold for use in the Caribbean in December 1994, following an extensive period of lay up at Leith. The little **Islander** remained on Orkney duties until August 1991, and was sold for further service in the Mediterranean in 1993.

The **Orcadia** *of 1962 departs Kirkwall for Orkney in March 1987. She eventually left the UK for a new career in the Caribbean in December 1994.*

The **Islander** *(1969) was clearly designed for cargo rather than passenger carrying, although she did have a certificate for twelve passengers. She was photographed as she arrived at Kirkwall, Orkney's capital.*

CHAPTER 12

TWIN AND TRIPLE SCREW VEHICLE FERRIES

The train ferries (Chapter 9) and the **Princess Victoria** and her successor on the Stranraer to Larne service (Chapters 5 and 8) paved the way for the modern roll-on roll-off stern loading vehicle ferry. The loss of the second **Princess Victoria** in 1953 was, however, a considerable set back to the introduction of the roll-on/roll-off concept in the UK, and it took the railways a further six years before they commissioned their next stern door ferry, albeit with steam turbine engines. Not so other UK operators and other nations; the Scandinavians were particularly active and innovative in the design and development of the vehicle ferry.

The single engine, single shaft concept was never used for the ever larger roll-on roll-off ferries. Popular with the North of Scotland, Orkney and Shetland Shipping Company, the last major ferry unit to depend on only one engine was their cargo and passenger ship **St Clair** which was completed in 1960 (Chapter 11). However, for a time the power available even from twin engines that would fit in the confined space beneath the car deck was insufficient for needs and resort to triple engines and shafts was made whilst engine design caught up.

The first of the new British stern-loading ferries was the **Bardic Ferry**, built in 1957 by William Denny for the Atlantic Steam Navigation Company, which was then part of the British Transport Commission. The launch of the new ship preceded that of the classic passenger and cargo ferry **St Clair** by three years, and the last classic passenger turbine steamer, the **Avalon**, did not arrive on station at Harwich until 1963! The Atlantic Steam Navigation Company had been set up before the war by Frank Bustard for cheap transatlantic passenger operation – a vision which was never realised. In post-war years, Bustard recognised the potential for using military Landing Ships Tank, with their front loading ramps, for commercial work. Starting with three steam reciprocating engined ships, the **Empire Baltic**, **Empire Cedric** and **Empire Celtic**, Bustard started a service between Tilbury and Rotterdam in September 1946. A service between Preston and Larne commenced in 1948 and the Tilbury base was subsequently transferred to Felixstowe. The company also traded as the Transport Ferry Service.

The **Bardic Ferry** was a highly innovative diesel stern loading freight and passenger ferry. The new ship bore little resemblance to the old landing craft. The engines were slightly forward of amidships and comprised two single acting 10-cylinder Sulzer units with an output of 2250 kW which at 250 revolusions per minute gave the ship a speed of 14 knots. As built, she was fitted with stabilizers. Possible military requirements necessitated a strengthened vehicle deck capable of carrying tanks and other heavy equipment and a clear headroom on the vehicle deck of 4.4 m. These features stood the **Bardic Ferry** and her later sisters in good stead as commercial vehicle axle loadings were soon to increase. There was space for 70 vehicles or trailers on the main vehicle deck, and containers could be loaded onto the upper cargo deck with the ship's own 20 tonne electric crane.

*The **Ionic Ferry** of 1958 is seen in the River Ribble below Preston Dock in September 1966. She is in as-built condition with electric crane on the aft deck.*

A new move for the company was the carriage of passengers. The passenger accommodation on the **Bardic Ferry** was of extremely high standard, and 55 passengers could be carried in two classes. First class comprised a twin berth suite forward of the funnel on the Sun Deck, and five single and five double berth staterooms on the Upper Deck, whereas second class comprised five double and seven four berth cabins on the Upper and Promenade Decks. The first class saloon was forward on the port side of the Upper Deck, and the second class saloon was on the starboard side. On the Promenade Deck the first class lounge was forward and the second class lounge was aft. Wood panelling was widely used in the public rooms to provide a feeling of warmth and comfort.

*The **Doric Ferry** (1962) sets out from Felixstowe in June 1967.*

*From a similar vantage point, we see the 1961-built **Cerdic Ferry** getting underway on 3 January 1975. The detail differences on the aft deck are very clear.*

The **Bardic Ferry** was launched at Dumbarton on 5 March 1957, and she entered service between Preston and Larne on 2 September, under the command of Captain H T Green. An identical sister, the **Ionic Ferry**, took up service at Preston on 10 October 1958 and the **Bardic Ferry** was then moved to the Tilbury to Antwerp route. So successful were the sisters that, in 1961 and 1962, the quasi-sisters **Cerdic Ferry** and **Doric Ferry** joined the fleet. These ships had less passenger accommodation and carried only 35 first class passengers in two- and four-berth cabins and one cabin de luxe. They were equipped with two 16-cylinder Paxman turbo charged engines which again sustained a service speed of 14 knots, with drive via a Modern Wheel oil operated 3 : 1 reverse reduction gearbox. Height clearance through the stern vehicle door was again 4.4 m and the maximum vehicle load that could be accommodated was 140 tonnes.

*The **Gaelic Ferry** (1963) arrives at Felixstowe in January 1975.*

The **Gaelic Ferry** followed in 1963, launched from Swan Hunter & Wigham Richardson's Tyneside yard on 3 October that year. She originally had accommodation for only 28 passengers (increased in 1972 to 44). Her engines were twin 10-cylinder Sulzer units, and these gave her a slightly faster speed of 16 knots. A stop-gap, converted former Landing Ship Tank, was bought at auction in Germany in 1965. Renamed **Celtic Ferry**, and capable of carrying 55 vehicle drivers, she retained her steam turbine engines. A freight only vessel, the **Baltic Ferry**, was also bought at about the same time, but this former Landing Ship Tank had been converted to diesel.

The final member of the class was the **Europic Ferry**, which was completed by Swan Hunter on 29 December 1967, ready to enter service between Felixstowe and Europort on 18 January 1968. She had accommodation for 44 passengers, and could carry 272 cars or 62 standard 12 m lorry trailers. There was a lower deck situated abaft the engine room and accessed by a hinged ramp from the main vehicle deck, and this was limited by headroom for use by export cars only. Her twin 16-cylinder SEMT Lindholmen-Pielstick engines provided a faster speed (18 knots) than that of the earlier ships, allowing her to complete the journey to Europoort in only six hours. Her crew complement was 52.

The former **Europic Ferry** *(1967) at Cairnryan in her final days under the Red Ensign as P & O's* **European Freighter** *on 2 April 1992.*

The **Europic Ferry** was one of the ships requisitioned for duty during the Falkland Islands war. Sailing from Portland on 25 April 1982, under the command of Captain Chris Clarke, she arrived at Port Stanley on 17 June, and eventually returned to Southampton on 17 July.

The ships passed into the fleet of the European Ferries Group in November 1971, and adopted the orange hull and green funnel of the Thoresen fleet in 1977. They later became part of the P&O group. As such, the **Europic Ferry** ended her days on the Cairnryan to Larne service for P&O (with an enlarged passenger certificate for 144), and for a short time carried the name **European Freighter**. The oldest four ships were sold for further service in the Mediterranean in the early 1980s, the **Gaelic Ferry** went directly for scrap in 1987, and the **Europic Ferry** joined her older sisters in the Mediterranean in 1992.

Another ferry operator to develope trade with converted military vessels was Townsend Brothers Ferries Limited. In post-war years, the converted River-class Frigate **Halladale** was used on the Dover to Calais route in competition with the railway's vehicle and passenger ferry **Lord Warden**. Both ships were steam turbine driven. The replacement for the **Halladale** was the **Free Enterprise**, a stern loading passenger and vehicle ferry capable of carrying 130 cars on two decks, or a combination of coaches, caravans and trailers. The central part of the vehicle deck had a headroom of 4.3 metres.

A classic view of the **Free Enterprise I** *(1962) as she sets out from Dover in April 1968.*

A contemporary account of the new ship by Commander R A B Kimpton, first published in *Sea Breezes*, November 1962, reports:

"Easy access from the car decks is gained to the passenger accommodation which is of contemporary design, and maximum comfort is provided in a spacious lounge. Abaft the lounge is a restaurant where all three meals are catered for at reasonable prices. At the fore end of the lounge are a buffet, shop and main bar. A service bar is also provided. Careful planning has obviously been employed and the accommodation is well lighted and ventilated."

The **Free Enterprise** had been built at Rotterdam by Werf Gusto at a cost of £1 million. Her twin 12-cylinder Smit MAN engines were coupled to feathering propellers so that bridge control was possible during docking. Her service speed was 19 knots. She entered service on 2 February 1962, having lain on the stocks for only eight months. The **Free Enterprise** was an immediate success; her light and airy open-plan accommodation contrasted with the alternative staid accommodation of the railway ships, and this appealed to the travelling public. Her external appearance was ultra-modern: Cunard Line cruise ship green hull topped by a thin red line and white superstructure, twin funnels abreast each other, red with a black top, modern streamlined superstructure and very clean lines. During the 18 years she was based at Dover, the **Free Enterprise** witnessed the complete evolution to the contemporary larger and faster second generation vehicle and passenger ferries. The **Free Enterprise** was the mother of them all.

The **Free Enterprise** *spawned a fleet of seven more Free Enterprise ferries. She adopted a suffix, to become the* **Free Enterprise I** *in 1964, ready for the arrival of the* **Free Enterprise II** *the following year. This was the first UK-registered drive through car ferry with both bow and stern loading, and was built at a cost of £1.3 million. She is seen in July 1968 as she passes through the eastern entrance to the port of Dover.*

The **Free Enterprise II** was the least successful of the ships, as she had a reduced vehicle deck headroom in response to lack of uptake on the service from commercial vehicles. As it happened, the uptake from commercial hauliers coincided with the delivery of the **Free Enterprise II**. The **Free Enterprise III** was also a one off ship; equipped with twin Smit MAN engines like the earlier pair, she also had two smaller non-reversible engines which could boost forward speed from 18 to 21 knots as required, working on the father and son principle.

The **Free Enterprise III** was highly successful on the Dover routes. However, for a few brief months in 1985, she became the Isle of Man Steam Packet Company's **Mona's Isle**. After she had been modified for her new owners, she suffered a deadweight problem which greatly reduced her carrying capability. Worse still, the **Mona's Isle** also suffered a number of 'total loss of control' incidents. At Dun Laoghaire, on her very first

visit in April 1985, she swung several times off the berth to the consternation of her master, Captain Vernon Kinley, before backing at great speed up to St Michael's Pier. One morning, she even ended up on the sands at Half Moon Bay, having missed the entrance to Heysham Harbour altogether, although she was soon able to reverse into deep water with the rising tide. Not surprisingly, her career as an Isle of Man boat was soon curtailed.

*The **Mona's Isle**, formerly the 1966-built **Free Enterprise III**, arrives at Heysham in September 1985 during her brief career as an Isle of Man vessel.*

The next ship, **Free Enterprise IV**, was a complete break from the mould. She was equipped with three propellers and three engines, much along the lines of the very early steam turbine ferries. This arrangement was necessary to provide the required propulsive power, there not being two sufficiently powerful engines available at that time that would fit beneath the vehicle deck. Again 12-cylinder Smit MAN engines were used, providing the ship with a very comfortable service speed of 19 knots. This same system was adopted for the subsequent fleet of the same class, each consecutively named up to **Free Enterprise VIII**, although each of the last three (**Free Enterprise VI**, **Free Enterprise VII** and **Free Enterprise VIII**) had three 8-cylinder Werkspoor TM410 type engines instead of Smit MAN.

*The **Free Enterprise V** (1970) at the eastern entrance to Dover harbour in September 1973.*

The various names adopted by these ships whilst under the Red Ensign, their tonnage and years of service are shown in Table 5.

*The second of the so-called "Super Vikings", the **Viking Valiant** of 1974, arrives at Portsmouth on 14 June 1984.*

The same triple screw, three engine arrangement was kept for the Thoresen quartet **Viking Venturer**, **Viking Valiant**, **Viking Voyager** and **Viking Viscount** built in 1974 and 1975 for the Southampton and Felixstowe routes. Built by Aalborg Værft A/S in Denmark, they had two 8-cylinder outer engines and a more powerful 9-cylinder central engine, all of the Werkspoor TM 410 type. Together these gave the ships a service speed of 18 knots. The subsequent trio **Herald of Free Enterprise**, **Spirit of Free Enterprise** and **Pride of Free Enterprise**, which joined the Dover to Calais service in 1979 and 1980, again had three engines, this time provided by Sulzer, type 2V/48 diesels, which gave them a speed of 23 knots. The system was retained for the **Pride of Calais** and **Pride of Dover**, which were delivered in 1987, each with three Sulzer engines on three shafts. No other British-registered ferries adopted this combination, the preferred option being four engines coupled to twin shafts.

A distinctive design was used for the **Norwave**, which inaugurated the new North Sea Ferries' overnight service between Hull and Rotterdam on 17 December 1965; she was later joined by her identical Dutch sister the **Norwind**. Built at Bremerhaven to the satisfaction of the owning consortium (two companies from each of Holland, Germany and the UK, the British companies being the General Steam Navigation Company and Tyne-Tees Steam Shipping Company), the ships had V314D Smit-Bolnes engines connected to twin shafts. They had a service speed of 16 knots, and were susceptible to heavy weather, with little reserve of power; heading into Force 7 would delay the ship anything up to 1½ hours.

*The **Norwave** (1965) manoeuvring in Hull's King George Dock during an evening departure in August 1967.*

Although only of 4038 tons gross, they had substantial accommodation for freight vehicles and cars (60 cars and 65 trailers or 200 cars), and a total passenger capacity of 235. There were berths for 187, mainly below the vehicle deck, and couchettes and reclining seats for the remainder. The fare included all meals whilst on board. The company also boasted fresh fruit in every cabin, a touch that set the service apart from others. The set breakfast had a rigid variety: bacon, sausage and egg fry into Rotterdam and bacon, tomato and egg fry into Hull!

Within the first six years of service, the **Norwave** and **Norwind** had put the Associated Humber Line's passenger service out of business (Chapter 11). In November 1972, North Sea Ferries announced plans for two new ships which were to be built by the same builder, A G Weser in Bremerhaven, and which would displace the earlier pair onto a new service between Hull and Zeebrugge. The new ships were the Hull-registered **Norland**, and the Rotterdam-registered **Norstar**. They were equipped with two 6750 kW Stork Werkspoor TM 410 engines coupled to independent shafts and had a service speed of 18.5 knots. Like the earlier pair, they were stern loading, but they had a much enlarged capacity for 1243 passengers and 139 freight units (or 200 cars).

The **Norland** was launched on 13 October 1973. The subsequent arrival of third generation ships in 1987, the **Norsea** and the Dutch registered **Norsun**, eventually displaced the **Norland** and her partner to the Zeebrugge service, allowing the original **Norwave** and **Norwind** to be sold for further service in the Mediterranean. Before taking up the Zeebrugge service, the **Norland** and **Norstar** were lengthened by just over 20 m. Cabin accommodation beneath the vehicle deck was given over to cargo space and the ships now offered 250 two- and four-berth en suite cabins, 96 two berth economy cabins and 42 reclining seats, and the total passenger complement became 881. They were finally displaced in 2001 by the new builds **Pride of Rotterdam** and **Pride of Hull**, at the time the world's largest ferries.

*The **Norland** (1974) has just entered the Humber from the lock and swings to port at the start of her voyage downriver in August 1974.*

The General Steam Navigation Company, conscious that its fleet of break-bulk coasting vessels had little future, was also instrumental in setting up another new consortium. This was Normandy Ferries, which inaugurated a new service between Southampton and Le Havre in 1967. Two identical sisters were built at

Dubigeon-Normandie in Nantes, the **Dragon**, registered at Southampton, and the **Leopard**, at Le Havre. The **Dragon** commenced service on 29 June 1967 in direct competition with Thoresen Ferries.

The **Dragon** dated from 1967 and is seen in the River Itchen at Southampton in June 1968. She is in as-built condition before additional cabin accommodation was constructed aft during the winter of 1968/69.

The **Dragon** was stern loading and could accommodate 276 cars or 60 by 12 m trailers. There was comfortable passenger accommodation for 846, with light and airy public rooms and a reputation for good quality catering. The ship was driven by twin 12 PC2V Pielstick engines which provided 6600 kW to maintain a service speed of 16 knots. P&O (the corporate head of General Steam Navigation Company) took over the service in due course, and the ships later also wore the colours of Townsend Thoresen when P&O sold out for £12.5 million in 1985. In July 1986, the **Dragon** was given the name **Ionic Ferry** and was transferred to the Cairnryan to Larne link where she worked alongside the **Europic Ferry** until sold in 1991. She was destroyed by fire in 2003.

Other first generation vehicle ferries were the last new builds for the Coast Lines Group: the **Ulster Prince** and **Ulster Queen** for the Belfast to Liverpool route, and the **Lion**, which took over the Ardrossan to Belfast service from the **Scottish Coast**, all in 1967. A contemporary description of the Liverpool boats which first appeared in the September 1971 issue of Sea Breezes reported:

"The **Ulster Prince** and **Ulster Queen** are twin screw vessels, propelled by two 12-cylinder Vee-type Crossley-Pielstick engines developing 5400 kW to give a service speed of 17.5 knots. For reversing each ship has a bow propeller. A total of 140 passengers' cars can be accommodated driving on and off through the stern loading door and ramp. There is accommodation for 1022 passengers in two classes, and each ship carries a crew of 85. A high standard of catering is maintained in the dining room on board these ships – a standard believed by many to be the finest of any of the Irish cross-channel routes."

The two Ulster ships suffered two fatal deficiencies. The first was that they had been designed with inadequate headroom on the vehicle deck to accommodate much of the commercial traffic on offer, and the second was that problems in Northern Ireland led to a downturn of trade in the 1970s. The difficulties were compounded by strikes, and when P&O took over the service in 1971, the writing was already on the wall. The ships were withdrawn in 1981, and were sold for further service in the Mediterranean.

The **Lion** was of quite different design, being a day ship for the Ardrossan service rather than an overnight ship. Like the **Ulster Queen**, she was built at Birkenhead by Cammell Laird & Company (the **Ulster Prince** had been built by Harland & Wolff at Belfast). She could carry 1200 passengers and up to 160 cars. Her twin Crossley 12-cylinder 4SC engines gave an output of 8750 kW and provided a service speed of 20 knots. Early on in her career, her reduction gearing gave problems, and she was eventually off service for part of the summer of 1971, during which period a variety of the steam turbine Isle of Man boats were used to maintain a skeleton passenger service. The **Lion** was later transferred from the ownership of Burns & Laird Lines to P&O in that same year, but the Ardrossan service was eventually terminated on 12 February 1976. The ship was moved to Southern Ferries (a trading partner of Normandy Ferries), for its service between Dover and Boulogne. In 1985 she became the Greek-flagged **Baroness M** and had an interesting charter for use as the **Portelet** for British Channel Islands Ferries in 1987 and 1988.

Although British Rail was not building diesel ferries through much of the 1960s, their Dutch and Belgian counterparts were entirely diesel. The first large diesel driven ferry for the railways since the **Cambria** and **Hibernia** of 1948 (Chapter 8) was the **Antrim Princess**. She was built by Hawthorn Leslie, and was launched into the Tyne on 24 April 1967. She was equipped with 16-cylinder Vee type Crossley-Pielstick engines, each of which weighed 70 tonnes, and which were coupled to twin controllable pitch propellers. Total output was 10,800 kW, which provided a service speed of 19.5 knots. She was also the first railway ship to be given the distinctive 'funnel on a funnel' which the railway design team gave to all its new build diesel ships over the ensuing ten years.

The **Antrim Princess** was designed for the short crossing between Stranraer and Larne. She was a drive-through ship with a bow visor. The vehicle deck could take 170 cars, or equivalent commercial vehicles with a maximum axle weight of 11 tonnes. She had berths for only 70 passengers, but as a day ship, she was licensed to carry 1200 passengers in two classes. She hit the headlines in December 1983, when an engine room fire left the ship without power in a storm, to the windward of Islandmagee. Passengers were lifted off by helicopter until sufficient power was eventually restored to bring the ship into Larne harbour. Between 1986 and 1980 she was transferred to the Isle of Man Steam Packet Company (then 40% railway owned) and operated as the **Tynwald**, but was later sold for further service in the Mediterranean.

A quasi-sister, the **Ailsa Princess**, was commissioned in 1971. She was built at Venice by the Breda Shipyard which had quoted a very competitive price of £2.5 million. She had the same engines, and virtually the same dimensions as the **Antrim Princess**, and the only major piece of equipment that differed was the steering gear. The Italians gave the funnel a continental flavour by extending the twin arrow logo around the whole circumference of the funnel and supporting the mainmast forward from the logo. The **Ailsa Princess** took up service at Stranraer in July 1971. She was ultimately displaced by the **Galloway Princess**, of the next generation of ferries, was renamed **Earl Harold** and was transferred to a variety of duties, mainly on the south coast. She was sold to Greek owners in 1990.

A new vehicle ferry for the Harwich to Hook of Holland service was the **St George**, also completed in 1967. Her specification included optimum machinery for a slow overnight passage outward and a faster daylight return – the obvious solution was a four-engined ship with the extra pair of engines only brought into use for the daylight service. The engines were 9-cylinder Ruston A O units which were bedded in pairs on two rafts, each pair connected into a gearbox also mounted on the raft with flexible couplings to the two shafts. They had a collective power of 13,500 kW to sustain the day crossing speed of 21 knots. However, at that speed, significant tail vibration was apparent in the first class accommodation which was situated aft. The night speed of only 17 knots was vibration free.

The **St George** could carry 205 cars, or combinations up to 34 commercial vehicles. As a day ship, she was certified to carry 1200 passengers, but on the night service she was restricted to just 600. Her consort was the Dutch-flagged **Koningin Juliana**, designed and built in the UK as a match for the **St George**. The pair maintained the service into the 1980s. They were joined in 1974 by the **St Edmund**, which replaced the classic steam turbine ferry **Avalon**, built only 11 years previously. The **St Edmund** was Sealink's largest ship to date, and was constructed by Cammell Laird at Birkenhead. She had four Stork Werkspoor engines, which drove twin controllable pitch propellers. She was designed with two class accommodation for 1000 night passengers and 1400 day passengers, with berths for 671, and airline seating for a further 150. The original crew requirement was 112.

The **St George** was displaced in 1983 by the arrival of the brand new **Princessan Birgitta**, which became the **St Nicholas**, and which eventually became Irish Ferries' Rosslare to Cherbourg vessel, the **Normandy**. The **St Edmund** was sent to the Falkland Islands war and, on return, was sold to the Ministry of Defence, and later served in a variety of roles including the **Rozel** for British Channel Islands Ferries in the early 1990s. As such she was a most comfortably appointed and spacious ship, as she was often only lightly loaded. It was a shame that at this stage of her career she was reduced to flying a flag of convenience.

A third railway ferry was built in the late 1960s. This was the **Vortigern**, essentially based on the **Antrim Princess** design, with the same arrangement of Pielstick engines and similar dimensions. She was designed for train ferry duties between Dover and Dunkerque, and doubled on the Dover to Boulogne vehicle ferry route as required. As a train ferry she operated as a stern loader with buffers forward on each of the four railway tracks. As a vehicle ferry she operated a drive through system and had portable mezzanine decks for cars. However, as originally built, she did not fit any of the local ramps, and had to be modified with the world's first 'cow catcher' ramp module designed and fitted to her bows by the Dover Engineering Department. In her early days her engines gave a lot of trouble with cylinder head joints blowing on a regular basis, as a result of coming up to the berth too fast and shutting down from full ahead too quickly. This problem was rectified by Pielstick in later engines. The traditional sewage trenches washed with sea water were needed for the Wagons Lits trains, and were accessed by a series of man-hole covers. A further problem was the combination of Wagons Lits with their anthracite stove heating and road vehicles with petrol fuel. This was overcome by damping down the stoves before they were shipped.

The **Vortigern** later served a variety of routes. The heavy construction of the train ferry saved her from almost certain destruction when she went ashore over a concrete groyne at Ostend in March 1984. She was floated off two days later, and was repaired at a cost of over £1 million. In 1988 she was withdrawn and sold for service in the Mediterranean.

Perhaps the most feted new build of this era was the **Spero**, a stern loading vehicle and passenger ferry built by Cammell Laird for the Ellerman's Wilson Line service between Hull and Gothenburg, as part of a three-ship consortium with two Swedish companies. All three ships, the **Spero**, and the Swedish **Svea** and **Saga**, were essentially similar. They had twin screws with twin engines geared to each shaft, in this case pairs of 6-cylinder Mirrlees Monarch engines. Collectively at 310 revolutions per minute, the arrangement produced 8200 kW, providing a speed of 18 knots.

Mini cruises were offered to Gothenburg on the three times a fortnight service. The four day mini-cruise aboard the **Spero** included sightseeing ashore and all meals, and cost between £22 and £38 per person depending on the grade of cabin. Her public rooms were described as of 'ocean liner standard' and included two spacious lounges, each with a bar, and one with a dance floor, and a restaurant and self service cafeteria. In addition there was a 'teenage room' complete with juke box, a sauna, and shops.

The **Spero** had a separate forward hold, as well as the vehicle deck. When built in 1966 she had the largest stern door of any British ferry, 5 m high by 9.4 m wide, which had been supplied by the MacGregor Corporation. Cars were loaded via a side door. She had berths for the total passenger complement of 408, and could also carry 100 standard containers and 100 cars. Sadly the odd combination of freight and freight vehicles saw the Gothenburg service fail in February 1971, but the ship was able to start a new service between Hull and Zeebrugge in April that year. Haplessly all she did then was develop trade for North Sea Ferries to take over when they switched the more appropriately configured **Norwave** and **Norwind** to this same route in 1974, rendering the **Spero** redundant.

The 1960s had seen a procession of new vehicle ferries of ever larger dimensions coming into service. The machinery progressed from single engine on each of twin shafts, flirted with father and son double engines on twin shafts (the **Free Enterprise III**), progressed to three engines, one on each of three shafts (**Free Enterprise IV** through to the **Pride of Calais**) and ended with the modern arrangement of twin engines on each of twin shafts. It was an interesting decade of ferry design that established the roll-on roll-off travel concept once and for all in British waters.

The state of the art was undoubtedly the **Antrim Princess** and the **St George**. That being so the three Irish ferries built for the state-owned British and Irish Steam Packet Company in 1969, the **Munster** and **Innisfallen** built at Rendsburg in Germany and the **Leinster** built by the Verolme Cork Dockyard at Rushbrook, County Cork, were perhaps the most fashionable. The ships were of Swedish design (indeed the **Munster** had a hull strengthened for navigation in ice), and had four MAN engines, which, at 430 revolutions per minute gave a speed of 22 knots. The coupling was two Renk gearboxes with multiplate clutches, which were pneumatically controlled from the engine room. Any combination of two, three or four engines could be brought into play as speed required. The three ships represented an investment of £7 million.

The trade mark of the three Irish ships was their "witch's hat" funnels and ultra modern appearance. Taking the **Leinster** by way of example, she was a one-class ship, with cabin accommodation for 1200 people, and there were two- and four-berth units for 252 passengers. Cabins beneath the vehicle deck were claustrophobic, noisy and hot, and it was not uncommon to find a structural pillar between bed and sink! There were 16 luxury cabins on the boat deck for the discerning few. The ship had two lounges with reclining seats for 325, there were three bars and a 63-seat restaurant, and a 300-seat cafeteria. The vehicle accommodation included hinged mezzanine decks for cars on either side of the main vehicle area. The three Irish ships were eventually displaced by second generation tonnage in the early 1980s.

The final entry of the decade was the magnificent **Blenheim**, built by Upper Clyde Shipbuilders at Govan in 1970 for Fred Olsen Lines (London) Limited at a cost of £4.5 million. Equipped with twin Crossley-Pielstick engines, she was registered in London, and was placed on their Harwich to Kristiansand summer service and the London to the Canary Isles winter cruise service. Built and registered in Britain, her owners benefited from investment grants that were then available to UK ship owners. At 10,420 tons gross, the **Blenheim** was the largest diesel ferry to date. She survived in various guises until 1996 when she was destroyed by fire.

ISLAND SERVICES

Few new buildings were completed in the 1960s specifically for island services because appropriate linkspans to connect vehicle ferries with islands had not, for the most part, yet been constructed. However, the side loading concept developed by the Caledonian Steam Packet Company in the 1950s was taken further by three side loaders built to the order of the Secretary of State for Scotland in 1964. These were the **Hebrides**, **Columba** and **Clansman**, which were managed and operated within the fleet of David MacBrayne Limited. They had twin screws driven by 8-cylinder Crossley type HRP8/47 engines, which gave them a speed of just over 14 knots. Maximum headroom on the vehicle deck was 3.3 m.

The three ferries were hugely successful and maintained a variety of Western Isles services. The **Columba** became the exclusive cruise ship **Hebridean Princess** in 1988, the **Hebrides** was sold in 1986 for use as the **Devoniun** out of Torquay, and later moved to Egyptian ownership. The **Clansman** was lengthened in 1972, and converted into a bow and stern door drive-through ship for use on the Ullapool to Stornoway route, on which she was not a success, and later on the Ardrossan to Brodick route, where she was given a better welcome. The vehicle deck headroom was increased by slicing the ship horizontally. The **Clansman** was sold in 1984.

Two rather remarkable vessels were built to the order of Western Ferries Limited, and were put into competition with David MacBrayne. These were the **Sound of Islay** (see page 59), which commenced a service between the seaward end of West Loch Tarbert and Port Askaig on Islay in April 1968, and her larger successor, the **Sound of Jura**, which took up station in July 1969, displacing the smaller ship to a new Campbeltown to Red Bay, County Antrim, service. The little **Sound of Islay** developed a magnificent following before the larger ship came into service. The **Sound of Jura** cost £0.3 million, was a drive through ship and included many innovative features. MacBraynes recognised the threat and deployed their own vehicle ferry to see the intruders away by 1975. The development lead of Western Ferries, nevertheless, hastened the deployment of drive-through tonnage in the Western Isles and served to highlight the role of Government subsidies to a preferred carrier, in this case David MacBrayne.

The state of the art in estuarine ferries was the **Cuthred**. Built in 1969 by Richards of Lowestoft, she had two Voith Schneider directional units, one fore and one aft, driven by two 8-cylinder Paxman engines. Double ended, like her predecessors on the Portsmouth to Fishbourne route, she was much bigger and had an improved underwater shape, requiring less power for the same speed. Her high windage proved a disadvantage, and later vessels (the **Caedmon**-class for the Lymington route), had a greatly reduced profile, and were better able to cope with adverse conditions. The **Cuthred** literally did "cut thread" in the Solent when her anchors pulled up the Isle of Wight telephone cable! With the arrival of the **St Helen** class of ferry in the early 1980s, the **Cuthred** became spare vessel, was laid up in 1986, and was eventually sold out of the fleet.

The distinctive lines of the **Sound of Jura** *(1969) are evident in this view of her arriving at Campbeltown from Red Bay in August 1970.*

TABLE 5 The Free Enterprise fleet, from the ownership of Townsend Brothers, through Townsend Thoresen and P&O European Ferries, to P&O-Stena Line and finally P&O Ferries

	UK service	Tons gross +	Comments
Free Enterprise	1962 - 1980	2606	Renamed *Free Enterprise I* 1964.
Free Enterprise II	1965 - 1982	4122	
Free Enterprise III	1966 - 1985*	4800	Sold to Mira Shipping, Malta in 1984, renamed *Tamira*.
Free Enterprise IV	1969 - 1988	5230	Renamed *Pride of Hythe* 1988.
Free Enterprise V	1970 - 1993	5049	Lengthened 1986, renamed *Pride of Sandwich* 1988, and
Free Enterprise VI	1972 - 1996	5049	*Pride of Ailsa* 1992.
Free Enterprise VII	1973 - 2000	5049	Lengthened 1986, renamed *Pride of Walmer* 1988, and *Pride of Rathlin* 1992.
Free Enterprise VIII	1974 - 1993	5200	Renamed *Pride of Canterbury 1988*
Viking Venturer	1974 - 2002	6387	Lengthened 1986. Renamed *Pride of Hampshire* 1989.
Viking Valiant	1974 - 2002	6387	Lengthened 1986. Renamed *Pride of Le Havre* 1989, and *Pride of Cherbourg* 1994.
Viking Voyager	1975 - 1994	6387	Renamed *Pride of Cherbourg* in 1989.
Viking Viscount	1975 - 1994	6387	Renamed *Pride of Winchester* in 1989.
Spirit of Free Enterprise	1979 - 2003	7951	Renamed *Pride of Kent* 1987, lengthened 1991/92, renamed *P&OSL Kent* 1999, and *P O Kent* 2002.
Herald of Free Enterprise	1979 - 1987	7951	Sank off Zeebrugge 6 March 1987 – 38 crew and 155 passengers lost.
Pride of Free Enterprise	1980 - 2000	7951	Renamed *Pride of Bruges* 1988, and *P&OSL Picardy* in 1999.
Pride of Dover	1986 -	26433	Renamed *P&OSL Dover* 1999, and *Pride of Dover* 2002.
Pride of Calais	1987 -	26433	Renamed *P&OSL Calais* 1999, and *Pride of Calais* 2002.

+   Tonnage as built

*   In 1985, operated as *Mona's Isle* for the Isle of Man Steam Packet Co Ltd. Sold after only six months in service following problems with deadweight.

CHAPTER 13

ECONOMIES OF SCALE

In 1970, the pride of the British ferry fleet was undoubtedly the foreign-owned **Blenheim**, which was then running seasonally out of Harwich for Fred Olsen (London) Ltd. She was soon to be overtaken by ships such as the **Eagle**, completed in 1972 for service between Southampton and Lisbon for Normandy Ferries. Sadly, the concept of a cruise ferry to Portugal was at least twenty years ahead of its time and this magnificent ship, branded as commercially unsuccessful, left the UK register after only 3 years service.

The 1972-built **Eagle** *of Normandy Ferries was a ship very much ahead of her time. She was photographed at Southampton in August 1973.*

The **Mona's Queen** *of 1972 is in the familiar setting of the River Mersey at Liverpool in September 1972.*

The move throughout the 1970s, and beyond, was largely based on economies of scale. With few exceptions, ever larger ships with ever more powerful propulsion units were coming off the drawing boards, all with a view to maximising their owners' profit margins. The exceptions included the two small side loading units built for the Isle of Man Steam Packet Company, a company which had finally realised that diesel propulsion could be a viable option for a passenger ferry, but could not quite throw off the traditional design for the new ships! These were the **Mona's Queen**, which came out in 1972, and her much loved, and surviving sister, the **Lady of Mann**, which was completed by the Ailsa Shipyard in 1976. These ships were powered by twin Crossley Pielstick engines, with 10 and 12 cylinders respectively, giving the **Lady of Mann** one extra knot service speed over her sister.

Certainly some important and impressive new tonnage was commissioned at this time for the premier ferry routes. Notable vessels, in addition to those mentioned in Chapter 12, were the British Rail/Sealink sisters **Hengist**, **Horsa** for the Folkestone and **Senlac** for the Newhaven stations, as well as the **St Columba** for Holyhead. The **Hengist** and her sisters had twin 16-cylinder SEMT Pielstick PC2V engines which sustained a service speed of just over 19 knots. The **St Columba**, later named **Stena Hibernia** and **Stena Adventurer**, the latter for a prospective move from Holyhead to Dover which never materialised, was similarly equipped, this time with twin 16-cylinder Stork Werkspoor TM410 engines, driving twin controllable pitch propellers via reduction gearing.

*The **Hengist** (1972) goes astern as she arrives at Folkestone in September 1973.*

*A powerful image of the **Senlac** (1972) setting out from Newhaven for Dieppe on 19 August 1973.*

An impressive drive-through vessel was built in 1973, to inaugurate the Irish Continental Line's new service between Rosslare and Le Havre. The **Saint Patrick** was completed at Rendsburg in Germany, and offered a single ship service, departing on alternate days from Rosslare at 1700 hours and from Le Havre the following afternoon at 1800 hours. The ship offered cabin accommodation for 550 passengers, ranging from two berth de luxe suites with bathrooms to four berth cabins with wash basins. The standard single passenger fares ranged in 1977 from £18.50 unberthed, up to £38. Displaced by larger second-hand tonnage from the Baltic, she was transferred to Belfast Car Ferries' new Liverpool to Belfast route in May 1982, six months after the 1967-built **Ulster Prince** and **Ulster Queen** had been withdrawn from the route (Chapter 12). In this role, she became the **Saint Colum**, and subsequently the **Saint Colum 1**, leaving Belfast at 2215 hours and returning from Liverpool (Langton Dock) the next morning at 1115 hours. She closed this route in September 1990, and was sold on for further service in Greek waters.

Operators in Scandinavia and the Mediterranean have always been more successful in maintaining the external appearance of their white-hulled fleets than their conterparts in the UK and Ireland. The **Saint Colum I** (1973), formerly the **Saint Patrick**, is in less than pristine condition as she enters the River Mersey from the Liverpool dock system at the start of a voyage to Belfast on 18 September 1985.

Wearing the livery of Sealink British Ferries, the **St Columba** (1977) leaves Holyhead for Dun Laoghaire on 30 July 1986.

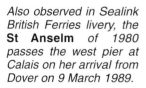

Also observed in Sealink British Ferries livery, the **St Anselm** of 1980 passes the west pier at Calais on her arrival from Dover on 9 March 1989.

By 1981, four interesting passenger and vehicle ferries emerged for Sealink, the **Galloway Princess** for Stranraer and the **St Anselm**, **St David** and **St Christopher** for Dover, although the **St David** was originally destined for Fishguard. They became the **Stena Galloway**, **Stena Cambria**, **Stena Caledonia** and **Stena Antrim** respectively when they were renamed by Stena Line in 1991. These ships still retained the system of a single engine on each of two shafts, and were given twin Crossley Pielstick 16-cylinder PC2V Mark V engines, similar to those on the **Hengist** class of vessels. At 520 revolutions per minute, the power output was 7600 kW, and this drove the ships at over 19 knots. The rebuilding programme finally ousted the turbine steamers from the Channel, a process that had only taken nine years to complete. Sadly, a number of Chief Engineers took early retirement, whilst others returned to deep sea service in order to be recertified for diesels. There was consequently an influx of new engineering staff at this time into the railway fleet, whilst this wealth of steam knowledge and experience was discarded. At the same time, remanning negotiations saw ships crewed up for 24 hour service, rather than the more customary shift service they had previously enjoyed. The turbine steamer **Invicta**, for example, had only been required to be in steam between 1200 and 1600 hours – an extremely leisurely existence by today's standards.

A feature of the 1970s and 1980s was the use of standard ships. These could either be ordered to a standard design, as were the **European Trader**, **European Gateway** and **European Clearway**, or customised from the same design as in the case of the **European Enterprise** (renamed **European Endeavour** in 1988). These freighters, with driver and limited passenger accommodation, served the Dover to Zeebrugge routes of Townsend Thoresen and later P&O. The **European Gateway** was lengthened in 1980, and her passenger certificate was increased from 52 to 326, for use on the Larne to Cairnryan service, but she was lost off Harwich after a collision with the train ferry **Speedlink Vanguard** in December 1982.

Photographed from the deck of the **Pride of Bruges** in June 1989, the **Baltic Ferry** (1978), complete with a temporary passenger module on the tank top, departs from Zeebrugge.

Standard ships were also built speculatively by some shipowners. The highly successful Stena Line **Sea Runner** design was also bought by Townsend Thoresen as second hand tonnage. Four ships, the **Cerdic Ferry**, **Doric Ferry**, **Baltic Ferry** and **Nordic Ferry**, came into the fleet in the 1980s, having been completed in the late 1970s at Ulsan in South Korea. They were stationed at Felixstowe, and later became the **European Freeway**, **European Tideway**, **Pride of Suffolk** and **Pride of Flanders** before the service was sold to Stena Line in 2002. In addition, the **Elk**, which unlike the others only has limited accommodation for 12 drivers, was originally chartered by P&O Ferrymasters when built, and was then bought for their service from Middlesbrough to Göteborg and Helsingborg. Typical of the class, the **Elk** is powered by two Pielstick 12PC2-5V-400 engines, connected to twin controllable pitch propellers. The total output is 11,474 kW, which provides the ship with a speed of over 18 knots. She joined DFDS Tor Line in 2000 as the **Tor Baltica**, but retained her British registry.

Three of the **Sea Runner** ships, the **Elk**, the **Nordic Ferry** and the **Baltic Ferry**, took part in the Falklands Islands war. The **Elk** was later lengthened to provide 1886 lane metres of freight space, and the two Prides were converted for passenger duties with the addition of a large

Passing the South Gare breakwater at the mouth of the River Tees, the 1978-built **Elk** heads for Gothenburg on 16 November 2000 shortly before adopting the name **Tor Baltica** after transfer to Harwich for DFDS Tor Line.

accommodation module for 688 passengers built forward of the bridge on the Main Deck. Installed in 1986, the passenger module was later removed in 1995, when the Felixstowe to Zeebrugge passenger service reverted to freight only. However, they can still carry over 160 drivers.

North Sea Ferries' **Norsea** and her Dutch-flagged sister **Norsun** are more notable new builds from the last two decades. The **Norsea** was the last major passenger unit to be built in the UK, and was completed by Govan Shipbuilders in 1987. Designed for the overnight Hull to Rotterdam passenger, vehicle and freight service, she was transferred to the Zeebrugge route in 2001 on the arrival of the **Pride of Rotterdam** and the **Pride of Hull**. The **Norsea** is equipped with the now commonplace arrangement of twin engines on each of two shafts, the engines being four sets of Wartsila Sulzer Type ZA 40 engines, which collectively produce 19 600 kW, providing a speed of 19 knots. As built, she could carry 1250 passengers, and 850 cars or 180 by 12 m trailers. She was given the corporate P&O Ferries name **Pride of York** in 2003; the **Norsun** then became the **Pride of Bruges**.

Typical of advances in freighter design was the **Baltic Eider**, with four cargo decks offering 2170 lane metres, or capacity for 390 12-metre trailers. She was built in Korea for the United Baltic Corporation in 1990 and was placed on the North Sea Services of the Finnanglia consortium, working out of Felixstowe. She is powered by Wartsila Type 46 medium speed oil engines arranged in a father and son pattern, with a 9-cylinder unit rated at 8145 kW and a 6-cylinder unit at 5430 kW, connected to a single controllable pitch propeller through a reduction gearbox to give the ship a speed of 19 knots.

P&O built four notable ships of the **European Seaway**-class in 1991 and 1992. Equipped with four Sulzer 8ZA40S engines each developing 5280 kW at 150 revolutions per minute, these ships were designed for the four hour Dover to Zeebrugge freight crossing to maintain a service speed of over 21 knots. The twin controllable pitch propellers are connected via a reduction gearbox. The **European Seaway** and her sisters, **European Highway** and **European Pathway**, accommodated 200 drivers in 43 outside two-berth cabins and 38 inside two-berth and Pullman third-berth cabins. They carried 124 by 15 m vehicles on two drive-through decks, the Upper Deck of 950 lane metres and the Main Deck of 975 lane metres, corresponding to a deadweight of 4600 tonnes on a draught of 6 metres. Each cost £50 million to build. The fourth ship was completed in 1993 as the **Pride of Burgundy**, with added accommodation for 1320 passengers on the Dover to Calais shuttle. All four ships were transferred to P & O Stena Line in 1998, and to P&O Ferries in 2002. The **European Highway** and **European Pathway** were converted for passenger use in 2003, becoming respectively **Pride of Kent** and **Pride of Canterbury**.

Three years later an even larger and faster pair of freight ferries was commissioned by North Sea Ferries for its overnight service between Hull and Europoort. These are the Dutch-registered **Norbank** and the Hull-registered (but now flagged out to Bermuda) **Norbay**. They have a twin father and son arrangement of 8- and 9-cylinder Sulzer 2A40S type engines, which give them a speed of 22 knots. These ships will passed into Stena Line management in 2004.

Even the estuarial and island ferries have grown in size. The Red Funnel Ferries' **Red Falcon** series of ships, built at Port Glasgow in 1994 and 1995 for the Southampton to Cowes service, have a gross tonnage of 2881. They are driven by two Stork Wartsila 8FHD 240 engines coupled directly to Voith Schneider cycloidal units, the first for the company since the **Vecta** was completed in 1939 (see Chapter 6). The total output of the machinery is 1195 kW at 778 revolutions per minute, giving the vessels a speed of 13 knots. Capacity is a mighty 890 passengers and 142 cars, 54 of them on the hoistable deck. The state of the art is Wightlink's new **St Clare**, offering capacity for 750 passengers and 180 cars, and driven by four Wartsila medium speed engines coupled to four Voith Schneider units. The **St Clare** cost £11.5 million to build, and entered service between Portsmouth and Fishbourne following delivery from her Polish shipbuilders in July 2001.

The last two decades of the twentieth century were still led by the principle of economies of scale. Rising fuel costs dictated that design and operational speeds were critical to the company balance sheet. Huge increases in fuel prices had taken place in 1973 as a result of Arab-Israeli conflict. Fuel economy was suddenly forced onto the agenda, and a series of innovative engine designs and engine features quickly emerged in response. One of the critical features was the ability of engines to burn heavier fuel of a poorer grade by incorporating sophisticated pre-heating systems to help vaporise the fuel. Another was the awareness of operators and marine engineers that one extra knot over 22 knots could require an extra fuel input of up to 25%.

That being so, the idea for very fast light twin hulled and mono-hulled craft, and the dawning of the Sea Cat era and the Stena HSS was inevitable. Offering a glamorous (if sometimes bumpy!) alternative to the conventional 'cruise ferry', these relatively small vessels have reduced journey times on some of the longer crossings in the western Channel and Irish Sea by one or two hours. In terms of payload and fuel consumption they are extremely inefficient, but these fast vessels have now developed their own following. Not so the gas-turbine driven Stena HSS class of vessel. Whereas these were relatively large vessels which stuck to the idea of the economies of scale, their dedicated shore terminals and the running costs of their gas-turbine engines have greatly inhibited their commercial success. Used on the Dun Laoghaire to Holyhead, Belfast to Stranraer and Harwich to the Hook routes, the Belfast vessel, the **Stena Voyager** burns 36 tonnes of relatively high octane fuel per round trip, whereas the conventional ferry **Stena Galloway** needed only 12 tonnes of cheaper heavy grade fuel oil.

There remains, and always will remain, a role for the conventional passenger and vehicle ferry. A modern development has been the combination of freight and passenger carrying, and a highly successful class of so called Ropax ships has been developed. These include the Isle of Man Steam Packet's **Ben-my-Chree**, and Irish Ferries **Isle of Inishmore** and **Isle of Innisfree**, the latter now the **Pride of Cherbourg** on charter to P&O Ferries at Portsmouth. These modern vessels all rely on twin diesel engine drive to each of twin shafts.

By way of example, the **Isle of Innisfree / Pride of Cherbourg** has four Sulzer 8ZAL40S on two shafts and a combined output of 23 040 kW. At 19 knots, the fuel consumption is 2.5 tonnes per hour, although the maximum speed available is 22.5 knots. With a capacity for 1650 passengers and three vehicle decks, which can carry 600 cars or combinations of cars and freight vehicles, she is big as well as fast. The **Isle of Inisfree** cost £46 million to build, and entered service between Dublin and Holyhead in the summer of 1995. She was transferred to the Rosslare to Pembroke Dock route on the arrival of the **Isle of Inishmore**, and was displaced by the arrival of the **Ulysses** in 2001, rendering her redundant at the age of six.

A disturbing trend during the 1990s was flagging out. In order for operators to maximise returns on ships, vessels were increasingly flagged out to the Bahamas and other registers of convenience, from which advantageous tonnage tax and other perks could be obtained. In a surprise move in 1995, P&O Pandoro decided to flag most of its fleet of vessels out to the Crown Dependency of Bermuda, maintaining, in the spin that followed this move, that the ships would still fly the Red Ensign. Conversely, and all things being relative, a number of Finnanglia vessels have been moved from the Finnish register to that of the UK, in order to benefit from apparently more relaxed taxation. Sea Containers also re-flagged their largely Bermudan fleet of Sea Cats to the UK. A further complication is the bareboat register, whereby the Irish-owned **Pride of Bilbao** was registered at Portsmouth, and the **Normandy**, until her purchase by Irish Ferries in 2000, was registered in Dublin. Nationality, it seems, does not necessarily reflect the seat of the Chairman and his Board.

Today the pride of the fleets must be Irish Ferries' **Ulysses** and the P&O North Sea sisters **Pride of Rotterdam** (Dutch flag) and **Pride of Hull**. The **Ulysses**, with a gross tonnage of 50,938 and a length overall of 209 m, is big indeed, and with a service speed of 22 knots she is also a fast ship. Propulsion consists of two pairs of MAK 9M 43 Resilient Mounted engines, which collectively provide 31 200 kW at 500 revolutions per minute, burning some 200 gm per kW per hour. The engines are protected by DICARE Engine Diagnostic System. The shafts are geared down to 145 revolutions per minute. Each propeller has a thrust of 1400 kN, is of the variable pitch type, and has four high skew blades.

The **Ulysses** offers an impressive 4076 lane metres of space on four vehicle decks, decks 1, 3, 5 and 7 and can accommodate 1342 cars or 240 freight units. The ship is serviced by a crew of 125, and can accommodate a total of 1875 passengers with a seat for everyone, as well as 111 twin berths and six single berths. Perhaps the most amazing statistic of the **Ulysses** is that her keel was laid at the Aker Finnyards in Finland on 24 January 2000 and she was launched on 1 September. Staggering also are the vessel's tank capacities (in tonnes):

Heavy fuel oil	1175
Diesel oil	137
Water ballast	4477
Heeling flume water	858
Lubricating oil	125
Fresh water	1137

At the turn of the century the **Ulysses** and the two P&O North Sea Ferries' Prides vied with each other for world's largest ferry. There must come a point when the optimal size is attained and ferries grow no more. Could these ships be that optimal design size? Only time will tell.

CHAPTER 14

TALES OF OLD

The SUCK-SQUEEZE-BANG-BLOW of the early internal combustion engine has evolved a long way to the sophisticated high speed marine diesel of the twenty first century. The contemporary design of engines is dictated by the need for speed (Stena Line claim that most passengers are bored after just two hours at sea!), economic operation, and ease of maintenance.

Amongst all this sophistication, the role of the **Ulster Monarch** and her sisters should not be forgotten. By contrast to modern ships, they were equipped with slow speed four-stroke cycle engines with everything monitored by eye, ear or touch, and all temperatures and pressures maintained by hand. Tales of her, and in particular of her war years, provide a fitting postscript to this story of the evolution of the diesel ferry and the universal adoption of the marine diesel engine.

The wartime activities of the **Ulster Monarch** (see Chapter 3) were broadly as follows:

September 1939: removed from her domestic ferry duties to carry troops of the British Expeditionary Force to France between Southampton and Le Havre or Cherbourg, and later Avonmouth to St Nazaire.

April 1940: carrying troops, munitions and fuel to Norway, then assisting with the evacuation, being the last merchant vessel to leave Harstad.

June 1940: refit on the Clyde, then to attend the evacuation of the British Expeditionary Force at Brest. To Casablanca and return to the UK via Gibraltar and Madeira. Occupation of Iceland and the Faroes, after which she returned to the UK.

October 1940: commissioned under the White Ensign as **HMS Ulster Monarch**. She became a part of the Combined Operations Fleet under Admiral Sir Roger Keyes, but continued with trooping duties to Iceland, Gibraltar and from there along the west coast of Africa as far as Lagos.

May/June 1942: fitted with assault craft for the North African landings.

August 1942: repairs at Liverpool followed by exercises with US Rangers and British Commandos.

November 1942: landed a complement of Rangers at the port of Arzeu; she then became the command centre for the area.

January 1943: attached to Force 'W'.

March 1943: to Gibraltar, then anticlockwise round Africa to Aden.

July 1943: through the Suez Canal to embark the SAS for transport to Sicily, landing them at the start of the invasion of Syracuse.

August 1943: carried troops and supplies between North African ports, Malta and Sicily. Attacked from the air, she retired to Tripoli for repairs.

September 1943: assault on Salerno.

December 1943: UK for refit.

June 1944: assault at Courseulles, and thereafter took up cross-Channel trooping duties.

September 1945: demobbed, and returned to her builders at Belfast for renovation to civilian life.

Her war service was courageous and valiant. She had sailed over 160,000 kilometres and carried over 200,000 men during the six years of hostilities. But what of the human aspects of life aboard **HMS Ulster Monarch**, and what was life like in the Engineering Department?

Ian Leafe joined the ship in 1942, at the age of 23, as an electrician. Discussion with him in recent years reveals the following insight to life in the Engineering Department during the ensuing war years. Ian recalls that, because many of the engineering crew were from opposite sides of the river in Glasgow, sectarian disagreements were commonplace. Soon after joining ship he was threatened by two of the crew who saw him as easy picking. Lying on his bunk, he refused their demands for ten shillings for beer, and under threat from the pair he swept his hand across the exposed bulkhead light into one of the faces. There was a greater respect for each other thereafter, and Ian was bothered no more.

Spare parts for the ship were always at a premium. The marine electrical spares were always sealed in zinc lined boxes to which a conductor was connected to an insulated terminal. In this way the condition of the part could be checked without opening the box. Eventually an armature was required to replace a faulty one and it was only then that it was realised that the inventory was amiss. Discussion with the **Ulster Queen** revealed that each had the other's stores, so a rendezvous was arranged in the Red Sea. Ian remarks:

"Imagine that after all those years from 1929 to 1943, and nobody had opened the boxes to check!"

Recalling the long haul round the Cape of Good Hope the ship had called at Gibraltar for bunkers and supplies, and set off for Freetown in company with a large convoy. For some reason, after dark, the funnel started to emit sparks as if it was Guy Fawkes Night and the Convoy Commodore was soon demanding that the **Ulster Monarch** stopped its display of illuminations. His message was dutifully reported to the Chief Engineer, Lieutenant Commander Kennedy, who was a colourful man of extremely wide girth. The reply was returned: what was he to do, sit on top of the funnel? To this came the reply from the Commodore: please do so if it will stop the sparks! Kennedy was the subject of much derision from his crew for quite a while thereafter!

Then there was the stretcher incident. Someone at the Admiralty had recognised the likelihood of the ship someday taking casualties (it was then nearly four years into the war!). A load of stretchers were taken on board whilst the **Ulster Monarch** was lying alongside the Govan Road in Glasgow, and these were hastily placed at strategic points about the ship. Even the generator room, with its vertical ladder access, was issued with one. Eventually the Medical Department decided it was time to test the stretchers, and a casualty was duly arranged in, of all places, the generator room. The volunteer was strapped to his stretcher so that only his eye lids could move, and then positioned on the main switch board landing. A dozen sailors waited on the boat deck to haul the casualty topside. Ian recounts:

"After a dozen checks the bosun gave the order Haul Away! And the stretcher started its vertical journey at increasing speed, as the deck crew found their pace. There was a jolt as the stretcher became snagged and the line came tight. Once free, the same order Haul Away! saw the stretcher accelerate upwards again only to snag once more. Cease Hauling! was ordered to release the stretcher as it came level with the upper coaming. The casualty arrived on the Boat Deck, blood streaming from his face, only to be rushed away by ambulance to the Great Northern Hospital on Lord Street with, it transpired, a cracked skull. His replacement was warned to keep well away from any stretcher!"

From the start, Ian was taken under the wing of one of the oilers, Ned Wallace. Ned was almost totally deaf and always refered to Ian as Young Un throughout their association. When the ship was in convoy under attack, Ned would come close up and say over the din "Oiy think thyere getting nearer!" If you could have heard the noise of the engines, depth charges, bombs and your own gunnery, there was clearly benefit in being nearly deaf. Ned was well over retirement age and, on return to the UK, was promptly put ashore. He returned to the pool and was soon back at sea, the only home he knew.

With regard to the bombing incident in August 1943, Ian reports almost casually:

"After the bomb hit the aft anti-aircraft gun, it went on down into the tiller flat and blew a hole out so one could get a closer view of the briny. There were four crew killed and the only survivor of the gun crew was the gunnery lieutenant. I was topside in the emergency generator room and, of course, the Gleniffer paraffin engine refused to start and we had no power for the pumps. I climbed down into the main engine room and it was a mess, for most of the decking plates had fallen down into the bilges and you had to tread on the supports. I could hear water running and soon got my back washed with hot water from a return line.

I spoke to the Chief Engineer for his orders, which were to try and get a generator going. I climbed back up to the Boat Deck and then down the fiddley to get to the generator room platform where I met up with a junior engineer called Paddy. I asked him what the situation was and he replied Bad. I asked him if he would go back down and pull all the wedges out of the main breakers and try to start a generator but not close any of the circuit breakers until I returned. We parted and I made my way up and aft to the stern, but the fire there was too hot. However, the fire crews had lots of water from the deck mounted pumps. Eventually, I got into the tiller flat and looked at the damage - the teller motors and hydraulic lines were OK, but a lot of cables near the distribution boxes were cut. I shortened the important ones up and rejoined those I needed for steering.

I returned to the generator room and the engineer had a generator running so I closed the circuit breaker for "C" masterboard down aft and went up to the bridge to ask the Quartermaster to give it some port and starboard helm in about ten minutes time. This allowed me to get to the tiller flat. I started the pumps for the teller motors - we had pressure, and then the quadrant moved the rudder as the Quartermaster turned the helm. I was satisfied it was working and returned to the bridge saluting the Captain: 'Sir we now have steering but I don't know how accurate the helm indicator will be!' I didn't bother the Chief Engineer as he had his hands full. Later we had main engines and headed for Tripoli. It all sounds so easy, but it was not really; the seamen had their own battles to do and an excellent job they did too.

Oh, I have to relate a humorous side for as I came up through the accommodation up to the Boat Deck there was a soldier lying on the stairway crying. I asked him 'Where have you been hit?' and he said 'I can't swim mate and I lost my life belt!' I said 'Here have mine but we're not sinking yet.' I popped into the emergency generator room for my spare belt I kept there but it was gone. I remember thinking he is a soldier? How on earth are we going to win the war? I often wondered if he survived!"

One of the more perverse stories Ian tells recalls the hatred of one of the engine room crew for one of the engineers:

"Before eight bells there is the single bell, the quarter, which alerts the next watch and gives the oncoming watch keeper time to confer as to the general situation in the engine room, such as valve grinding or oil make up on the purifiers. The engine room crew came via B Deck, whereas the engineers were in the midcastle accommodation on the Boat Deck. The engineers commonly entered the fiddley on the Boat Deck and slid down the rails to the domestic boiler flat, then a right turn and another slide down the rails to the control area. Now, the engineer who was to take the midnight watch fell sick, and a change was made. The other engineer slid down the rails into a line tied between the rails at a stanchion sending the victim head over heels into the auxiliary equipment around the domestic boiler. I often wondered if his colleague had known what was in store for him, or if indeed he was the intended victim."

On the sailing ability of **HMS Ulster Monarch**, Ian reports that, with a clean bottom, she was fit for 21 knots, and on a hard turn she would heel over almost like a destroyer. Using both engines and the rudder her ability to turn saved the ship often when avoiding mines. In rough weather she would bury her forecastle completely and the forward well deck would be flooded before she would shudder and shake her head, shedding the unwanted load. If the weather was either from the port or the starboard quarter she was a good sea vessel with a twisting motion given to the saying: one hand for the ship and one hand for yourself.

"I used to read as I lay on my bunk. She would start to heel over and I used to hear a creak, which all ships have, but this one said that she had gone as far over as needed, then the creaking groan would stop and I knew she was righting herself. I am not positive after so many years but I think the maximum on the inclinometer was 38° during the great hurricane in the Bay of Biscay when we did only 37 kilometres in 24 hours. Nevertheless, I liked the ship very much.

The Donkey Man, Chris Murphy a scouser, joined the ship when she was commissioned in 1929 and stayed with her until she was scrapped – she cannot have been that bad a ship! As for Ian Leafe, he left the ship at Belfast when she was decommissioned and pursued a successful career in diesel engine commissioning in Canada and the Middle East.

For my part, I remember the **Ulster Monarch** slowly emerging out of the early morning mist and gloom, having turned through 180° to come alongside ahead of Princes Lock to face the incoming tide and the lock entrance. Bleary eyed passengers line the Boat Deck railings, some perhaps wondering why a boy should have cycled through the dark of the night to photograph their dawn arrival. As the forecastle rises in the lock and becomes temporarily level with the quay, the morning newspapers are hauled aboard. As the ship slowly moves off down the dock system towards her berth at Princes, the sun finally rises over the sheds to give the camera a fighting chance.

Romantic images apart, the final word must lie with Harland & Wolff and a delightful Union-Castle Line anecdote. This story comes from Ian Ramsay, Secretary to The Institution of Engineers and Shipbuilders in Scotland and is about a friend's father who had served his apprenticeship ashore at Belfast with Harland & Wolff. This man first went to sea on the maiden voyage of the very first diesel driven liner in the Union-Castle fleet, the **Carnarvon Castle**, in 1926. At the same time, the Union-Castle Line's Commodore Chief Engineer was making his very last voyage before retirement, and this was to be his only voyage in a motor ship. Apparently, the venerable gentleman spent almost the entire voyage to the Cape and back looking in total horror at the 16-cylinder clattering diesel engines, and saying to all and sundry in a broad Belfast accent – "Is it any wonder that Dr Diesel committed suicide?"

APPENDIX 1

BRITISH AND IRISH NEW BUILDS – SMALL DIESELS, LARGE DIESELS AND TURBINE STEAMERS

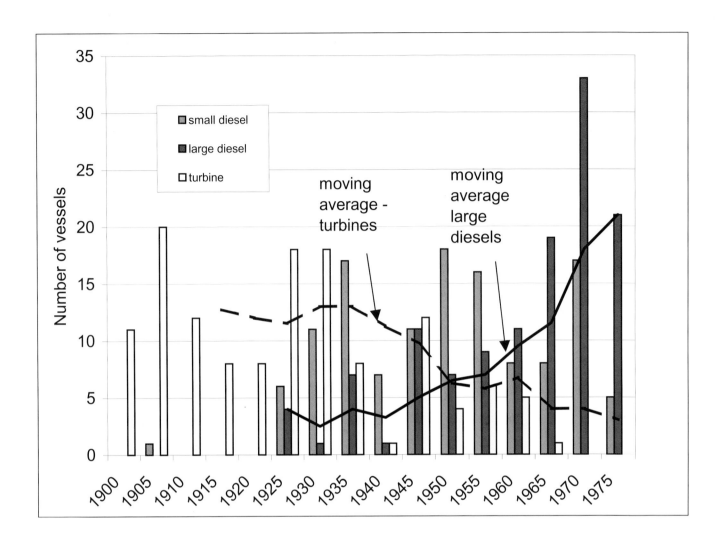

The chart shows the new builds between 1900 and 1980 of British and Irish passenger carrying short sea vessels. There are three categories: small diesels, i.e. less than 1000 tons gross, large diesels and turbine steamers. The columns show the actual number of ships in each category built within the five year period shown. Also, the twenty year moving average for both turbine steamers and large diesels is shown. These show the average number of new builds per five year period across the twenty year period following.

The chart shows a number of features:

* There has been a general decline in the number of small diesels commissioned relative to large diesels because island and estuarine ferries have become larger to satisfy demand.

* Right from the late 1920s onwards, when the **Ulster Monarch** and her sisters were commissioned, the twenty year moving averages show an inevitable decline in turbine steamers and a rise in large diesels.

* The overall number of new builds has steadily increased from the late 1930s onwards.

APPENDIX 2

EARLY DEVELOPMENT OF TWO-STROKE AND FOUR-STROKE ENGINES BY SULZER

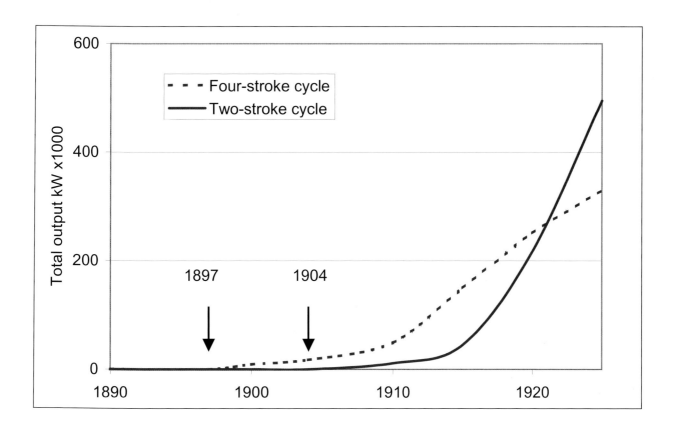

The total output of marine diesel engines built by Sulzer at their works in Winterthur, Switzerland, by 1925 was 450,000 kW, or about 600,000 brake horse power. The first four stroke cycle engines produced by the company came out in 1897 and the annual increase in production of these had already started to decline by 1925. The two stroke cycle engine was first manufactured by Sulzer in 1904 and production increased exponentially from about 1910 onwards. By 1925, the largest engines were producing up to 7,500 kW.

*The Sulzer-engined **Elk** (1959) is seen in Southampton Water without passengers on a routine trip from the Channel Islands in May 1970.*

BRITISH AND IRISH MOTOR FERRIES OVER 130 TONS GROSS COMMISSIONED UP TO 1970

Details are as first built or as first commissioned into the UK Merchant Service. Foreign flag vessels built before 1970 and subsequently bought by a British flag company are not included. Date of scrapping or of loss is given where known, the ship may well have been sold prior to this date. Ownership of vessels in the period since 1970 is complicated by bareboat charters and leasing arrangements – see contemporary shipping catalogues for details.

Name	Dates	Grt	Speed (Knots)	Engine builder

Associated Humber Lines Limited
Hull and Goole to Rotterdam, Antwerp, Ghent and Copenhagen services

Name	Dates	Grt	Speed	Engine builder
Bolton Abbey	1958-1983	2706	15	Ruston and Hornsby
Byland Abbey	1957-1980	1372	13	Ruston and Hornsby
Fountains Abbey	1954-1962	1197	13	Kincaid-Polar
Kirkham Abbey	1956-1983	1372	13	Ruston and Hornsby
Melrose Abbey	1958-1980	2500	15	Ruston and Hornsby
Whitby Abbey	1954	1197	13	Kincaid-Polar

*An attractive water-level view of the **Melrose Abbey** (1958), reproduced from an offical company postcard.*

(Bernard McCall collection)

Atlantic Steam Navigation Company Limited
Preston to Larne and Belfast, Tilbury to Antwerp and Rotterdam

Name	Dates	Grt	Speed	Engine builder
Bardic Ferry	1957-1988	2550	14	Sulzer
Cerdic Ferry	1961	2563	14	Paxman
Doric Ferry	1962	2563	14	Paxman
Europic Ferry	1967	4190	18	SEMT Lindholmen-Pielstick
Gaelic Ferry	1963-1987	2754	16	Sulzer
Ionic Ferry	1958-1988	2548	14	Sulzer

Belfast Steamship Company Limited
Liverpool to Belfast

Name	Dates	Grt	Speed	Engine builder
Ulster Monarch	1929-1966	3735	18	Burmeister & Wain
Ulster Prince	1930-1941	3735	18	Burmeister & Wain
Ulster Prince	1967	4270	17	Crossley-Pielstick
Ulster Queen	1930-1950	3735	18	Burmeister & Wain
Ulster Queen	1967	4270	17	Crossley-Pielstick

Birkenhead Corporation
Liverpool to Birkenhead

Mountwood	1960	464	12	Crossley
Overchurch	1962	468	12	Crossley
Woodchurch	1960	464	12	Crossley

British & Irish Steam Packet Company Limited
Liverpool to Dublin, Swansea to Cork

Innisfallen	1969	4849	23	MAN
Leinster	1937-1967	4302	18	Harland & Wolff B&W Type
Leinster	1948-1987	4115	17	Harland & Wolff B&W Type
Leinster	1969	4849	22	MAN
Munster	1938-1940	4302	18	Harland & Wolff B&W Type
Munster	1948-2000	4088	17	Harland & Wolff B&W Type
Munster	1969	4067	22	MAN

*The **Leinster** (1969) was in her first year of service when photographed arriving at Liverpool during the summer of 1969.*

British Transport Commission
Holyhead to Dun Laoghaire, Stranraer to Larne, Portsmouth to Ryde, Dover to Dunkerque and Boulogne, Harwich to Zeebrugge and Hook of Holland, Southampton and Weymouth to the Channel Islands, Portsmouth to Fishbourne, Lymington to Yarmouth, Tilbury to Gravesend, Skye ferry.

Antrim Princess	1967	3630	19	Crossley-Pielstick
Brading	1948-1995	837	14	Sulzer
Camber Queen	1961	293	10	Crossley
Cambria	1948-1980	4972	21	Harland & Wolff B&W Type
Cambridge Ferry	1963-2003	3294	13	Mirrlees National
Catherine	1961	214	9	Lister Blackstone
Cuthred	1969	704	10	English Electric
Edith	1961	214	9	Lister Blackstone
Elk	1959-1976	795	14	Sulzer
Essex Ferry	1956-1984	3242	13	Sulzer
Fishbourne	1961-1985	293	10	Crossley
Freshwater	1959-1997	350	10	Crossley
Hibernia	1948-1981	4972	21	Harland & Wolff B&W Type
Kyleakin	1970	225	8	Gardner
Moose	1959	795	14	Sulzer
Norfolk Ferry	1951-1983	3137	13	John Brown
Rose	1961	214	9	Lister Blackstone
St George	1967	7356	21	Ruston
Shanklin	1951-1981	833	14	Denny-Sulzer
Southsea	1948	837	14	Sulzer
Vortigern	1969	4371	19	Crossley-Pielstick

Burns & Laird Lines Limited
Glasgow to Belfast, Londonderry and Dublin, Ardrossan to Belfast

Lairds Loch	1944-1970	1580	13	British Auxiliaries
Lion	1967	3333	20	Crossley
Royal Scotsman	1936-1984	3244	17	Harland & Wolff B&W Type
Royal Ulsterman	1936-1973	3244	17	Harland & Wolff B&W Type

The 1967-built **Lion** *at Ardrossan on 16 July 1969.*

Caledonian Steam Packet Company Limited
Firth of Clyde services

Arran	1954-1993	568	15	British Polar
Arran Mail	1936-1962	137	10	Gleniffer
Bute	1954-1983	570	15	British Polar
Caledonia	1966	1156	19	MAN
ex-*Stena Baltica* (Swedish) 1969				
Cowal	1954-1984	569	15	British Polar
Glen Sannox	1957-2000	1107	18	Sulzer
Iona	1970	1192	16	Paxman
Maid of Argyll	1953	508	15	British Polar
Maid of Ashton	1953	508	15	British Polar
Maid of Cumbrae	1953	508	15	British Polar
Maid of Skelmorlie	1953	508	15	British Polar

City of Cork Steam Packet Company Limited
Fishguard to Cork

Innisfallen	1930-1940	3071	18	Burmeister & Wain
Innisfallen	1948-1985	3705	17	Harland & Wolff B&W Type

Clyde Navigation Trust
Govan and Finnieston ferry, upper Clyde

Vehicular Ferryboat No 4				
	1938-1976	250		Davey-Paxman+

Coast Lines Limited
Liverpool to London and Middlesbrough, Glasgow to Dublin, Irish Sea relief services

Aberdonian Coast	1946-1975	1258	14	British Polar
Atlantic Coast	1934-1973	890	12	British Auxiliaries
British Coast	1933-1981	890	12	British Auxiliaries
Caledonian Coast	1948-1974	1265	14	British Polar
Irish Coast	1951-1989	3813	17	Harland & Wolff B&W Type
Ocean Coast	1935-1969	1173	11	British Auxiliaries
Pacific Coast	1935-1940	1210	11	British Auxiliaries
Pacific Coast	1947-1977	1188	12	British Polar
Sark Coast	1945-1963	318	10	Davey-Paxman
ex-*LCG(M) 196* (British) 1949				
Scottish Coast	1957-2002	3817	17	Harland & Wolff B&W Type

Commodore Cruises Limited
Guernsey to Alderney and Sark

Island Commodore	1942	195	9	Crossley
ex-*TRV 2* (British) 1950				

Coras Iompair Eireann
Galway to Aran Islands

Naom Éanna	1958	483	10	British Polar

S R Crowe
Brighton excursions

Regency Belle	1942	251	10	General Motors Corporation
ex-*Radcliffe* (American) 1950				

Currie Line Limited
Leith to German and Danish ports

Zealand	1955	2030	12	British Polar

William Denny & Brothers Limited
North Queensferry to South Queensferry

Mary Queen of Scots	1949-1964	230	11	Crossley #
Queen Margaret	1934-1964	228	8	Davey-Paxman + #
Robert the Bruce	1934-1964	228	8	Davey-Paxman + #
Sir William Wallace	1956-	277	8	Crossley #

Devon Cruising Company Limited
Torbay excursions

Bateau Morgat	1953	152	8	Deutz
ex-*Morgat* (French) 1964				

Down County Council
Strangford to Portaferry

Strangford Ferry	1969	186	10	Kelvin

Dundee Harbour Trustees
Newport to Dundee

Abercraig	1939-1986	455	9	Brush Electrical Engineering
Scotscraig	1951-1980	463	9	English Electric

Ellerman's Wilson Line Limited
Hull to Scandinavian Ports, Harwich to Hook of Holland (for Ministry of Transport)

Aaro	1960-1984	2468	13	Fairfield-Sulzer
Cavallo	1951-1980	2340	13	British Polar
Empire Wansbeck	1942-1980	3562	16	MAN
ex-**Linz** (German) 1945				
Spero	1966	6916	18	Mirrlees Monarch
Trentino	1951-1980	2340	13	British Polar

*The **Spero** (1960) is seen in the King George V Dock at Hull on departure to Zeebrugge in July 1968.*

Mr Jack Ellis
Scarborough excursions

Coronia	1935	227	13	National Gas & Oil

Forth Ferries Limited
Granton to Burntisland

Bonnie Prince Charlie	1943	469	12	Davey-Paxman
ex-**LCT 4-673** (British) 1950				
Eriskay	1943	384	12	Davey-Paxman
ex-**LCT** (British) 1950				
Flora Macdonald	1943	469	12	Davey-Paxman
ex-**LCT 893** (British) 1950				
Glenfinnan	1944-1955	468	12	Davey-Paxman
ex-**LCT 1048** (British) 1950				

General Steam Navigation Company Limited
Thames area excursions

Queen of the Channel	1949-1984	1472	19	Sulzer
Royal Daffodil	1939-1967	2060	21	Sulzer
Royal Sovereign	1948	1851	20	Sulzer

Gosport Ferry Company
Gosport to Portsmouth

Gosport Queen	1966	159	10	Gardner
Portsmouth Queen	1966	159	10	Gardner

The **Gosport Queen** *(1966) off Gosport on 19 April 2003.*

Isles of Scilly Steamship Company Limited
Penzance to Scilly

Queen of the Isles	1965-1997	515	13	Ruston and Hornsby
Scillonian	1956	921	15	Ruston and Hornsby

The Liverpool and North Wales Steamship Company Limited
North Wales Excursions

St Silio	1936-1975	314	13	Crossley

London, Midland & Scottish Railway
Stranraer to Larne, Windermere excursions

Princess Victoria	1939-1940	2197	19	Sulzer
Princess Victoria	1946-1953	2694	19	Sulzer
Swan	1938	251	11	Gleniffer
Teal	1936	251	11	Gleniffer

London & North Eastern Railway
Clyde ferry services and excursions, Harwich to Zeebrugge

Suffolk Ferry	1947-1981	3134	13	John Brown
Talisman	1935-1967	544	17	British Polar + #

Mac Shipping Company Limited
Clyde excursions

Wimaisia	1936	309	9	Harland & Wolff +
ex-*Duchess of Abercorn* (British) 1948				

David MacBrayne Limited
Scottish Western Island and Clyde services

Clansman	1964	2104	14	Crossley
Claymore	1955-2000	1024	12	Sulzer
Columba	1964	2104	14	Crossley
Hebrides	1964	2104	14	Crossley
Loch Arkaig	1942-1985	179		Bergius
ex-*MMS* (British) 1959				
Loch Carron	1951	683	11	British Polar
Lochdunvegan	1946	528	10	Atlas
ex-*Örnen* (Dutch) 1950				
Lochearn	1930-1983	542	9	Gardner Denver
Lochiel	1939-1995	580	14	Paxman-Ricardo
Lochfyne	1931-1974	748	16	Davey-Paxman +
Lochinvar	1908-1966	188	12	L Gardner & Sons *
Lochmor	1930-1969	542	9	Gardner Denver
Lochnevis	1934-1969	568	15	Davey-Paxman +
Loch Seaforth	1947-1973	1089	14	Sulzer

The 1964-built **Columba** *was registered initially at Leith under the ownership of the Secretary of State for Scotland but managed by David MacBrayne Limited.*

New Medway Steam Packet Company Limited
Thames area excursions

Queen of the Channel	1935-1940	1162	19		Sulzer
Rochester Queen	1944	309	10		Davey-Paxman
ex-*LCG(M) 181* (British)	1948				
Royal Sovereign	1937-1940	1527	21		Sulzer

North of Scotland, Orkney & Shetland Shipping Company Limited
Services to Orkney and Shetland Islands, Shetland inter-island services

Earl of Zetland	1939	548	12	British Auxiliaries
St Clair	1960-1987	3302	13	Sulzer
St Clement	1946-1984	460	12	British Polar
St Ninian	1950-1991	2242	15	British Polar
St Ola	1951-1987	750	12	British Polar
St Rognvald	1955	1024	13	Sulzer

North Sea Ferries Limited
Hull to Rotterdam

Norwave	1965-1988	4038	16	Smit-Bolnes

Fred Olsen Lines (London) Limited
Harwich to Kristiansand and London to Canary Islands

Blenheim	1970-1997	9248	22	Pielstick

*The 1970-built **Blenheim** was very much a state-of-the-art vessel when seen arriving at Harwich in August 1974.*

Orkney Islands Shipping Company
Orkney inter-island services

Islander	1969	250	11	Paxman
Orcadia	1962	869	12	British Polar

Pembrokeshire County Council
Pembroke Dock to Neyland

Cleddau King	1962	151	9	Gleniffer

Thomas Round & Sons
Scarborough excursions

New Royal Lady	1939-1994	248	14	Crossley
Royal Lady	1934-1942	195	12	Crossley

Ross and Cromarty County Council
South Kessock to North Kessock

Rosehaugh	1967	150	8	Bergius Kelvin

Shannon Ferry Limited
Killimer, Co. Clare to Tarbert, Co. Kerry

Shannon Heather	1968	300	9	Perkins

Southampton, Isle of Wight and South of England Royal Mail Steam Packet Company Limited
Southampton to Cowes, excursions

Balmoral	1949	688	15	Newbury-Sirron
Carisbrooke Castle	1959	620	14	Crossley
Cowes Castle	1965	786	14	Premier
Medina	1931	347	10	L Gardner & Sons
Norris Castle ex-*LCT* (British) 1948	1942	473	9	Davey-Paxman
Norris Castle	1968	734	14	Premier
Osborne Castle	1962	736	14	Crossley
Vecta	1938-1997	630	15	English Electric

Southern Ferries Limited (Normandy Ferries)
Southampton to Le Havre

Dragon	1967-2003	5720	16	Pielstick

Southern Railway
Portsmouth to Fishbourne, Lymington to Yarmouth, Southampton to Channel Islands

Farringford	1947-1984	489	10	Crossley + #
Fishbourne	1927-1964	136	8	L Gardner & Sons
Hilsea	1930-1961	149	18	L Gardner & Sons
Lymington	1939-1996	295	11	W H Allen
Winchester	1947-1996	1149	15	Sulzer
Wootton	1928-1962	154	8	L Gardner & Sons

Townsend Brothers Ferries Limited / Townsend Car Ferries Limited
Dover to Calais and Zeebrugge

Free Enterprise	1962	2606	19	Smit MAN
Free Enterprise II	1965	4122	19	Smit MAN
Free Enterprise III	1966	4800	21	Smit MAN
Free Enterprise IV	1969	5230	19	Smit MAN
Free Enterprise V	1970	5049	19	Smit MAN

United Baltic Corporation Limited
London to Baltic ports

Baltabor	1924-1939	2592	12	Gotaverken
ex-**City of Panama** (American) 1937				
Baltavier	1924-1964	2592	12	Gotaverken
ex-**City of San Fransisco** (American) 1937				

Wallasey Corporation
Liverpool to Seacombe and New Brighton, excursions

Egremont	1951	566	14	Crossley
Leasowe	1951	567	14	Crossley
Royal Daffodil II	1958	608	12	Crossley
Royal Iris	1950	1234	13	Ruston+

Western Ferries Limited
West Loch Tarbert to Islay, and Campbeltown to Red Bay

Sound of Islay	1968	280	10	Kelvin
Sound of Jura	1969	519	14	Lister Blackstone

Woolwich Free Ferry (London County Council)
North to South Woolwich

Ernest Bevin	1963	739	8	Mirrlees Blackstone
James Newman	1963	739	8	Mirrlees Blackstone
John Burns	1963	739	8	Mirrlees Blackstone

* paraffin engines
+ electric coupling
# paddle wheel

The **Ernest Bevin**, of 1963, photographed in mid-Thames during April 1994.

REFERENCES

Periodicals

Journal of Commerce; *Marine Propulsion International*; *Motor Ship*; *Sea Breezes*.

Books

Brodie I 1976. *Steamers of the Forth*. David & Charles, Newton Abbot.

Brown A 1979. *Craigendoran Steamers*. Aggregate Publications, Johnstone.

Cameron S 2002. *Death in the North Channel, the loss of the **Princess Victoria** January 1953*. Colourpoint Books, Newtownards.

Danielson R 1999. *The Honourable Balmoral, Her Peers and Piers*. Maritime Publications, Laxey, for Waverley Excursions Limited.

Dendy Marshall C F 1936. *A History of the Southern Railway*. The Southern Railway Company, London.

Duckworth C L D & Langmuir G E 1956. *West Coast Steamers*. 2nd edition. T Stephenson & Sons, Prescot.

Duckworth C L D & Langmuir G E 1967. *West Highland Steamers*. 3rd edition. T Stephenson & Sons, Prescot.

Duckworth C L D & Langmuir G E 1967. *Railway and Other Steamers*. 2nd edition. T Stephenson & Sons, Prescot.

Duckworth C L D & Langmuir G E 1972. *Clyde River and Other Steamers*. 3rd edition. Brown, Son and Ferguson, Glasgow.

Duckworth C L D & Langmuir G E 1977. *Clyde and Other Coastal Steamers*. 2nd edition. T Stephenson & Sons, Prescot.

Farr G 1967. *West Country Passenger Steamers*. 2nd edition. T Stephenson & Sons, Prescot.

Guthrie J 1971. *A History of Marine Engineering*. Hutchison, London.

Liddle L 1998. *Passenger Ships of the Irish Sea*. Colourpoint Books, Newtownards.

Robins N S 1995. *The Evolution of the British Ferry*. Ferry Publications, Kilgetty.

Robins N S 1998. *The British Excursion Ship*. Brown, Son and Ferguson, Glasgow.

Robins N S 1999. *Turbine Steamers of the British Isles*. Colourpoint Books, Newtownards.

Sinclair R C 1990. *Across the Irish Sea, Belfast-Liverpool Shipping Since 1819*. Conway Maritime Press Ltd., London.

Thornley F C 1962. *Past and Present Steamers of North Wales*. 2nd edition. T Stephenson & Sons, Prescot.

Thornton E C B 1962. *South Coast Pleasure Steamers*. T Stephenson & Sons, Prescot.

Thornton E C B 1972. *Thames Coast Pleasure Steamers*. T Stephenson & Sons, Prescot.

Wrigley T F 1946. *MV **Ulster Monarch** - the Story of a Proud and Gallant Ship*. Ulster Imperial Line, Belfast.

*Back cover photograph : Although not ideally suited for conditions in the Irish Sea which at times can be "lively", the **Container Enterprise** and her sistership **Container Venturer**, both dating from 1958, were pioneering vessels as discussed on page 66. The **Container Enterprise** was photographed at her usual berth on the North Quay at Heysham on 30 September 1978.*

(Bernard McCall)

SHIP NAME INDEX

Names in ordinary typescript are British and Irish motor ferries or excursion ships. Names in italics are steam ships or motor ships of other nationalities.

Aaro (1960) 64,110
Aba (1918) 5
Abercraig (1939) 41,46,110
Aberdonian Coast (1946) 55,109
Adda (1922) 6,9
Adrias (1937) 32
Ailsa Princess (1971) 61,91
Al Khairat (1960 82
Angelo (1957) 64
Antrim Princess (1967) 90,91,92,107
Anzio I (1908) 11
Aphrodite (1948) 51
Apollo (1936) 31
Arctic Star (1936) 31
Ariosto (1956) 64
Arran Mail (1936) 37,108
Arran (1954) 71,72,108
Ashton (1938) 37
Atlantic Coast (1934) 54,55,109
Autocarrier (1948) 52,53
Avalon (1963) 84,91

Balmoral (1949) 69,114
Baltabor (1924) 33,115
Baltavia (1924) 33,115
Baltic Eider (1989) 99
Baltic Ferry (1943) 85
Baltic Ferry (1978) 98
Bardic Ferry (1957) 7,84,85,106
Baroness M (1967) 90
Bateau Morgat (1953) 109
Batory (1936) 34
Ben-my-Chree (1966) 8
Ben-my-Chree (1998) 100
Bermuda (1927) 13
Berry Castle (1922) 12
Blarna (1961) 72
Blenheim (1970) 92,95,113
Bolton Abbey (1958) 81,106
Bonnie Prince Charlie (1943) 74,110
Bournemouth Queen (1935) 38,58
Brading (1948) 68,69,107
Brian Boroime (1970) 66
Brightlingsea (1925) 12
Brighton (1931) 14
Bristol Queen (1938) 37
Brit (1935) 37,38
Britannic (1930) 14,15
British Coast (1933) 54,55,109
Brittany (1933) 57
Broadford (1953) 72
Buccaneer (1950) 76
Bury (1910) 81
Bute (1954) 71,72,108
Byland Abbey (1957) 57,64,106

Caedmon (1973) 93
Caledonia (1966) 108
Caledonian Coast (1948) 55,56,109

Caledonian Princess (1961) 48,66
Calshot (1930) 73
Calshot (1964) 73
Camber Queen (1961) 73,107
Cambria (1948) 46,48-50,78,90,107
Cambridge Ferry (1963) 62,65,107
Cammell Laird (1936) 31
Carabinier (1878) 10
Carisbrooke Castle (1959) 73,114
Carnarvon Castle (1926) 103
Carrick Coast (1933) 66
Carrick Lass (1934) 13
Catherine (1961) 75,107
Cavallo (1951) 64,100
Celtic Ferry (1944) 85
Cerdic Ferry (1961) 85,106,120
Cerdic Ferry (1977) 98
Cheshire Coast (1954) 56
Chimu (1924) 33
Cill Airne (1962) 73
City of Hydra (1955) 79
City of Panama (1924) 33,115
City of San Fransisco (1924) 33,115
Ciudad de Asunciun (1930) 35
Clansman (1964) 23,93,112
Classic (1893) 13,16
Claymore (1955) 23,27,79,112
Cleddau King (1962) 114
Columba (1878) 10
Columba (1964) 93,112
Comet (1905) 5,10,11
Commodore Queen (1944) 74
Container Enterprise (1958) 66,116
Container Venturer (1958) 66
Continental Queen (1935) 39
Coronia (1935) 37,58,110
Coronia (1935, ex Brit) 38
Countess of Breadalbane (1936) 37
Cowal (1954) 71,72,108
Cowes Castle (1965) 73,114
Crested Eagle (1939) 38
Cumbal (1924) 33
Cuthred (1969) 93

Darlington (1958) 66
Dartmouth Higher Ferry (1960) 45
Devonia (1956) 80
Devoniun (1956) 80
Devoniun (1964) 93
Dextrous (1956) 45
Director (1956) 45
Dittisham Castle (1922) 12
Doric Ferry (1962) 85,106,120
Doric Ferry (1977) 98
Dover (1965) 50
Dragon (1967) 90,114
Duchess of Abercorn (1936) 75,112
Duchess of Hamilton (1932) 36
Duchess of Montrose (1930) 36
Duke of Lancaster (1928) 17

Eagle (1972) 95
Earl Harold (1971) 61,91
Earl of Zetland (1939) 40,76,77,113
Earl Sigurd (1931) 82
Earl Thorfinn (1928) 82
Edith (1961) 75,107
Egremont (1951) 69-71,115
Elk (1959) 57,105,107
Elk (1978) 98
Empire Baltic (1945) 84
Empire Cedric (1944) 84
Empire Celtic (1945) 84
Empire Parkeston (1930) 53
Empire Wansbeck (1939) 53,110
Empire Wave (1941) 30
Empress Queen (1940) 39
Epping (1914) 12
Eriskay (1943) 74,110
Ernest Bevin (1963) 115
Esperos (1939) 53
Essex Ferry (1917) 64
Essex Ferry (1956) 65,107
European Clearway (1976) 98
European Endeavour (1978) 98
European Enterprise (1978) 98
European Freeway (1977) 98
European Freighter (1967) 86
European Gateway (1975) 98
European Highway (1992) 99
European Pathway (1992) 99
European Seaway (1991) 99
European Tideway (1977) 98
European Trader (1975) 98
Europic Ferry (1967) 86,90,106

Falaise (1946) 46
Farringford (1947) 44,45,114
Fife Coast (1933) 66
Fishbourne (1927) 12,73,114
Fishbourne (1961) 73,107
Flora Macdonald (1943) 74,110
Fountains Abbey (1954) 57,64,106
Free Enterprise (1962) 86,87,94,114
Free Enterprise I (1962) 86,87,94
Free Enterprise II (1965) 87,94,114
Free Enterprise III (1966) 7,87,88, 92,94,114
Free Enterprise IV (1969) 10,88,92, 94,114
Free Enterprise V (1970) 88,94,114
Free Enterprise VI (1972) 88,94
Free Enterprise VII (1973) 88,94
Free Enterprise VIII (1974) 88,94
Freshwater (1959) 45,73,107

Gaelic Ferry (1963) 85,106
Galaxias (1957) 79
Galloway Princess (1980) 91
Galway Bay (1930) 73

Gatcombe (1960) 73
Gay Queen (1938) 37
Georgic (1931) 14,15
Glanmire (1936) 66,107
Glen Sannox (1957) 58,72,108
Glenamoy (1916) 6
Glenapp (1918) 5
Glenartney (1915) 6
Glenfinnan (1944) 74,110
Golden Eagle (1909) 4,52
Gosport Queen (1966) 111
Gradely (1905) 10
Graphic (1906) 13,30

Hainault (1914) 12
Halladale (1944) 86
Hebridean Princess (1964) 93
Hebrides (1964) 23,93,112
Hemelata (1943) 74
Hengist (1972) 96
Herald of Free Enterprise (1979) 88,94
Heroic (1906) 13,50
Hibernia (1948) 46,48-50,78,90,107
Hibernian Coast (1946) 55,56
Highland Hope (1928) 13
Highland Monarch (1928) 14
Hilsea (1930) 12,73,114
Horsa (1972) 96
Hotspur II (1937) 37
Hotspur III (1938) 37

Ile de Serk (1942) 75
Imperial Eagle (1939) 38
Innisfallen (1930) 16,17,19,35,108
Innisfallen (1948) 19,51,108
Innisfallen (1969) 8,92,107
Invicta (1940) 46
Iona (1970) 59,108
Ionic Ferry (1958) 84,85,106
Ionic Ferry (1967) 90
Ioulis Keas II (1958) 71
Irish Coast (1951) 19,20,46,77,78,109
Ischia (1948) 52
Island Commodore (1942) 75,109
Islander (1969) 82,83,113
Isle of Inishmore (1997) 100
Isle of Innisfree (1995) 100

James Newman (1963) 115
Jersey Queen (1944) 74
John Burns (1963) 115
Juno (1912) 9
Jutlandia (1911) 5

Kalundborg (1931) 35
Keppel (1961) 75
Kilkenny (1937) 67
King Edward (1901) 36
King George V (1926) 10,36
Kirkham Abbey (1956) 57,64,106
Koningin Emma (1939) 33-35
Koningin Juliana (1968) 91
Kronprins Frederik (1940) 35

Kyleakin (1930) 12
Kyleakin (1960) 72
Kyleakin (1970) 107

Lady Ailas (1934) 13
Lady Connaught (1906) 50
Lady of Mann (1976) 95
Lairds Isle (1911) 30,78
Lairds Loch (1944) 46,108
Lairdsbank (1936) 66,67
Lairdscrest (1936) 66
Lairdsglen (1954) 57
Lairdsgrove (1898) 30
Lairdshill (1921) 57
Lairdsrock (1898) 30
Lairdswood (1936) 66
Lancashire Coast (1954) 56
Lancastria (1922) 17
Leasowe (1951) 69-71,115
Leinster (1937) 19,30-32,50,107
Leinster (1948) 19,49-51,55,107,120
Leinster (1969) 92,107
Leopard (1967) 90
Leven (1938) 37
Lincoln Castle (1940) 45
Linz (1939) 53,110
Lion (1967) 31,90,108
Loch Arkaig (1942) 74,112
Loch Carron (1951) 47,57,112
Loch Eynort (1947) 74,75
Loch Seaforth (1947) 7,47,79,112
Lochalsh (1957) 13,72
Lochdunvegan (1946) 57,112
Lochearn (1930) 11,21-23,25,27,79,112
Lochfyne (1931) 6,22-24,27,36,42,112
Lochiel (1939) 25-27,47,80,112
Lochinvar (1908) 5,10,11,112
Lochmor (1930) 11,21-23,25,27,112
Lochness (1929) 21
Lochnevis (1934) 24-27,42,112
Lochshiel (1929) 21
Longford (1906) 50
Lord Warden (1952) 48,86
Lymington (1939) 41,44,45,73,114

Magic (1893) 16
Maid of Argyll (1953) 71,108
Maid of Ashton (1953) 71,108
Maid of Bute (1937) 37
Maid of Cumbrae (1953) 71,108
Maid of Skelmorlie (1953) 71,108
Makalla (1948) 56
Malabar (1925) 13
Maldive Importer (1956) 64
Marchioness of Graham (1936) 36
Marchioness of Lorne (1935) 44
Mary Queen of Scots (1949) 42,109
Medina (1931) 36,114
Medway Queen (1924) 11
Melrose Abbey (1958) 81,106
Mersey Coast (1938) 3,55
Moil (1936) 13
Mona's Isle (1966) 87,88,94
Mona's Queen (1972) 95
Mons Abyla (1931) 36

Moose (1959) 57,107
Morgat (1953) 109
Mountwood (1960) 71,107
Munster (1938) 19,30-32,35,107
Munster (1948) 19,49-51,55,107
Munster (1969) 61,92,107

Naom Éanna (1958) 75,109
New Royal Lady (1939) 37,114
Nishika Maru (1934) 35
Norbank (1993) 99
Norbay (1994) 99
Nordic Ferry (1978) 98
Norfolk Ferry (1951) 64,65,107
Norland (1974) 62,89
Normandy (1982) 91,100
Normannia (1952) 46
Norris Castle (1942) 74,114
Norris Castle (1968) 73,114
Norsea (1987) 89,99
Norstar (1974) 89
Norsun (1987) 89,99
Norwave (1965) 89,92,113
Norwest Laird (1939) 26,80
Norwind (1966) 89,92

Ocean Coast (1935) 54,55,109
Odysseus (1937) 32
Oia (1949) 52
Orcadia (1962) 82,83,113
Örnen (1946) 57,112
Orpheus (1948) 51
Osborne Castle (1962) 73,114
Overchurch (1962) 71,107

P&OSL Calais (1987) 94
P&OSL Dover (1986) 94
P&OSL Kent (1979) 94
P&OSL Picardy (1980) 94
Pacific Coast (1935) 54,55,109
Pacific Coast (1947) 55,56,109
Patriotic (1912) 13
Pin Mill (1910) 12
Portelet (1967) 90
Portree (1951) 72
Portsmouth Queen (1966) 111
Poseidonia (1948) 51
Pracaxa (1944) 74
Prapida (1943) 74
Pride of Ailsa (1972) 94
Pride of Bilbao (1986) 4,100
Pride of Bruges (1980) 94
Pride of Bruges (1987) 99
Pride of Burgundy (1993) 99
Pride of Calais (1987) 88,92,94
Pride of Canterbury (1974) 94
Pride of Cherbourg (1974) 94
Pride of Cherbourg (1975) 94
Pride of Dover (1986) 88,94
Pride of Flanders (1978) 98
Pride of Free Enterprise (1980) 88,94
Pride of Hampshire (1974) 94
Pride of Hull (2001) 89,99,100
Pride of Hythe (1970) 94

Pride of Kent (1979)	94
Pride of Le Havre (1974)	94
Pride of Portsmouth (1990)	4
Pride of Rathlin (1973)	94
Pride of Rotterdam (2001)	89,99,100
Pride of Sandwich (1972)	94
Pride of Suffolk (1978)	98
Pride of the Bay (1938)	37
Pride of Walmer (1973)	94
Pride of Winchester (1975)	94
Pride of York (1987)	99
Prince Baudouin (1934)	29,30,35
Prince Ivanhoe (1951)	68,69
Prince Phillippe (1939)	29
Princess Amarosa (1957)	79
Princess Beatrix (1939)	33,34
Princess Margaret (1931)	30,47
Princess Victoria (1939)	7,33,35,111
Princess Victoria (1946)	7,46-48,84,111
Princessan Birgitta (1982)	91
Prins Albert (1937)	29,30
Prinses Beatrix (1939)	34
Queen Emma (1939)	34
Queen Margaret (1934)	42,109
Queen Mary (1933)	36,39
Queen of Scots (1935)	38,58
Queen of the Channel (1935)	35,38,39,113
Queen of the Channel (1949)	4,52,111
Queen of the Isles (1965)	80,111
Radcliffe (1942)	109
Rapallo (1960)	66
Red Falcon (1994)	99
Regency (1951)	78
Regency Belle (1942)	74,109
Remvi (1956)	80
Rhodri Mawr (1970)	66
Riviera (1911)	30
Robert the Bruce (1934)	42,109
Rochester Queen (1944)	74,113
Rose (1961)	75,107
Rosehaugh (1967)	114
Royal Daffodil (1939)	39,52,111
Royal Daffodil (1958)	70,71
Royal Daffodil (1962)	71
Royal Daffodil II (1958)	69,70,115
Royal Eagle (1932)	38,52
Royal Iris (1950)	60,69-71,115
Royal Iris of the Mersey (1960)	71
Royal Lady (1934)	35,114
Royal Lady (1939)	38,74
Royal Scotman (1936)	31
Royal Scotsman (1936)	19,30-32,34, 35,106,108
Royal Sovereign (1937)	35,39,113
Royal Sovereign (1948)	52,53,111
Royal Ulsterman (1936)	19,30-32, 34,66,108
Rozel (1974)	91
St Anselm (1980)	63,97,98
St Christopher (1981)	98
St Clair (1960)	81,82,84,113
St Clair II (1960)	82
St Clare (2001)	99
St Clement (1946)	56,76,77,113
St Columba (1977)	96,97
St David (1981)	98
St Edmund (1974)	91
St George (1967)	91,92,107
St Helen (1983)	93
St Nicholas (1982)	91
St Ninian (1950)	76
St Ola (1951)	76,77,113
St Patrick (1947)	57
St Rognvald (1955)	56,113
St Silio (1936)	37,38,111
St Trillo (1936)	38
Saga (1966)	92
Saint Colum (1973)	96
Saint Colum I (1973)	96,97
Saint Columba (1911)	24
Saint Patrick (1973)	96,97
Santa Catalina (1924)	33
Santa Monica (1924)	33
Sark Coast (1945)	74,109
Scillonian (1927)	79
Scillonian (1956)	79,80,111
Scillonian III (1967)	80,81
Scotscraig (1951)	41,46,110
Scottish Coast (1957)	19,78,79,90,109
Scout (1907)	5,10,11
Sea Freightliner I (1968)	66
Sea Freightliner II (1968)	66
Selandia (1911)	5
Senlac (1972)	96
Shanklin (1951)	68,107
Shannon Heather (1968)	114
Shieldhall (1955)	4
Shun Siung (1924)	33
Sir William Wallace (1956)	42,109
Skellig (1947)	75
Slieve Donard (1959)	66
Snaefell (1906)	30
Sound of Islay (1968)	59,93,115
Sound of Jura (1969)	93,115
Sound of Sanda (1939)	41
Sounion (1936)	31
Southern Coast (1911)	54
Southsea (1948)	68,69,107
Speedlink Vanguard (1973)	98
Spero (1966)	92,110,120
Spirit of Free Enterprise (1979)	63,88,94
Stella Polaris (1927)	29
Stena Adventurer (1977)	96
Stena Antrim (1981)	98
Stena Baltica (1966)	108
Stena Caledonia (1981)	97
Stena Cambria (1980)	96,97
Stena Hibernia (1977)	96
Stena Voyager (1996)	100
Storebælt (1939)	35
Strangford Ferry (1969)	109
Suffolk Ferry (1947)	64,65,112
Surendra (1943)	74
Svea (1966)	92
Swan (1938)	37,111
Syllingar (1956)	80
Talisman (1935)	7,36,42-44,112
Tamira (1966)	94
Teal (1936)	37,111
Theseus (1948)	51
Toiler (1911)	9
Tor Baltica (1978)	98
Train Ferry No 2 (1917)	64
Train Ferry No 3 (1917)	64
Trentino (1951)	64,110
Ulster Monarch (1929)	7,14-19,32,34,35, 36,60,77,101-103,106
Ulster Prince (1930)	14-17,19,32,35,106
Ulster Prince (1937)	19,32,50,77
Ulster Prince (1967)	90,96,106
Ulster Prince I (1937)	32
Ulster Queen (1930)	14-17,19,35,101,106
Ulster Queen (1967)	8,90,96,106
Ulster Weaver (1936)	67
Ulysses (2001)	100
Valonia (1947)	74
Vandal (1904)	9
Vecta (1938)	7,40,41,99,114
Vega (1938)	29,35
Vehicular Ferryboat No 4 (1938)	25,108
Venus (1931)	29,35
Viceroy of India (1929)	7
Vienna (1929)	53
Viking Valiant (1974)	88,94
Viking Venturer (1974)	88,94
Viking Viscount (1975)	88,94
Viking Voyager (1975)	88,94
Viper (1906)	30
Vortigern (1969)	91,107
Vulcanus (1910)	9
Wakefield (1958)	66
Waverley (1947)	44,58,69
Wee Cumbrae (1935)	37
West Leyte (1954)	64
Westward Ho (1938)	41
Whitby Abbey (1954)	57,64,106
William Gregson (1936)	75
Wimaisia (1936)	75,112
Win (1905)	10
Winchester (1947)	6,57,114
Winston (1955)	56
Woodchurch (1960)	71,107
Wootton (1928)	12,73,114
Wyre Lady (1938)	37
Yorkshire Lady (1935)	38
Zealand (1955)	64,109

IN LATER YEARS

Buyers in the Mediterranean have long purchased ferries from northern Europe and have usually succeeded in obtaining several more useful years service from each vessel. Indeed some of these ferries have been the subject of investment to make them more suitable for their intended market. All photographs were taken by Bernard McCall in the Piraeus area in August 1984.

Even after earning their keep in waters far from the original routes, all ferries reach the end of their working life. The **Aphrodite** *was amongst a host of laid-up ships anchored off Perama when photographed on a rather hazy day. She began life at the Harland & Wolff yard in Belfast in 1949 and was originally the* **Leinster** *of the British & Irish Steam Packet Company Ltd. She left northern Europe in 1969 after being briefly renamed* **Leinster I** *to free her original name for a new vessel.*

Certainly not laid up is the elegant **Sappho***, originally the* **Spero** *of Ellerman's Wilson Line. Built by Cammell Laird at Birkenhead in 1966, she worked from the UK for only seven years and was an excellent purchase for her Greek owners.*

The lines of the **Atlas II** *are unmistakable. She was originally the 1962-built* **Doric Ferry** *of the Atlantic Steam Navigation Company Ltd. She left the fleet in 1981 along with the* **Cerdic Ferry** *which became* **Atlas I***. The ships were built at the Ailsa yard in Troon.*